© Alberto Tolot

ANSEL ADAMS *at* 100

JULY 9–NOVEMBER 3, 2003

Ansel Adams at 100 has been organized by The San Francisco Museum of Modern Art.

The international tour is made possible by Hewlett-Packard.

Support for the MoMA showing is provided by AOL Time Warner Book Group and the Robert and Joyce Menschel Family Foundation.

Additional funding is provided by the Daniele Agostino Foundation.

The accompanying educational programs are made possible by BNP Paribas.

MoMA**QNS**   The Museum of Modern Art, Queens

33 ST. AT QUEENS BLVD., LONG ISLAND CITY, QUEENS (212) 708-9400 WWW.MOMA.ORG   SUBWAY: 7 LOCAL TO 33 ST. MONDAY, DAILY 10:00 A.M.–5:00 P.M., FRIDAY 10:00 A.M.–7:45 P.M., CLOSED TUESDAY AND WEDNESDAY

Ansel Adams. n.d. Gelatin Silver Print. Collection Ansel Adams Archive, Center for Creative Photography, University of Arizona. © Rondal Partridge.

FRONT COVER: Henri Cartier-Bresson, New York City, 1947.

EUGÈNE ATGET'S TREES
NEWLY DISCOVERED PHOTOGRAPHS FROM
THE BIBLIOTHÈQUE NATIONALE DE FRANCE

D.A.P./ DISTRIBUTED ART PUBLISHERS, INC.

Slipcased, 11.25 x 16.25 inches
96 pages / 39 tipped-on tritones
$125 ISBN 1-891024-67-1

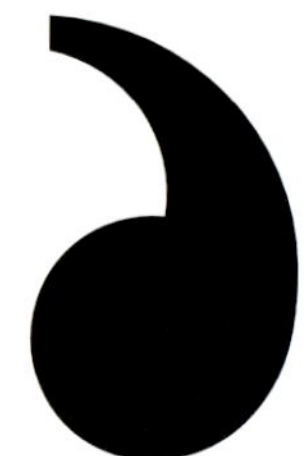

d·a·p

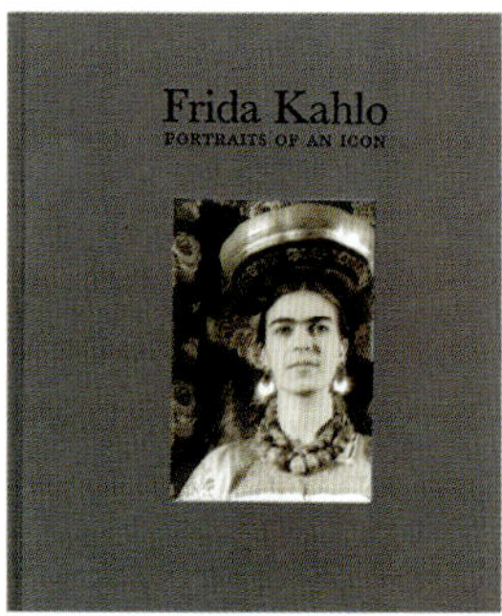

FRIDA KAHLO
PORTRAITS OF AN ICON
TURNER

Clothbound, 9.5 x 12.5 inches
152 pages / 59 tritones
$65 ISBN 84-7506-564-3

BRUCE DAVIDSON
A TIME OF CHANGE: CIVIL RIGHTS
PHOTOGRAPHS 1961-1965
ST. ANN'S PRESS

Clothbound, 12 x 11 inches
172 pages / 140 tritones
$65 ISBN 0-9713681-1-2

WINOGRAND
FIGMENTS FROM THE REAL WORLD
THE MUSEUM OF MODERN ART, NEW YORK

Clothbound, 11 x 10.25 inches
260 pages / 208 duotones
$55 ISBN 0-87070-635-7

ARNOLD ODERMATT
KARAMBOLAGE
STEIDL

Hardcover, 9.5 x 12.5 inches
400 pages / 410 duotones
$65 ISBN 3-88243-866-5

PHILIP-LORCA diCORCIA
THE MUSEUM OF MODERN ART, NEW YORK

Hardcover, 10.5 x 9.5 inches
80 pages / 55 color
$24.95 ISBN 0-87070-145-2

JOEL STERNFELD
TREADING ON KINGS
PROTESTING THE G8 IN GENOA
STEIDL

Paperback, 9 x 11 inches
90 pages / 40 color
$20 ISBN 3-88243-837-1

TOM HUNTER
HATJE CANTZ PUBLISHERS

Flexibound, 9.25 x 11 inches
80 pages / 50 color
$30 ISBN 3-7757-1277-1

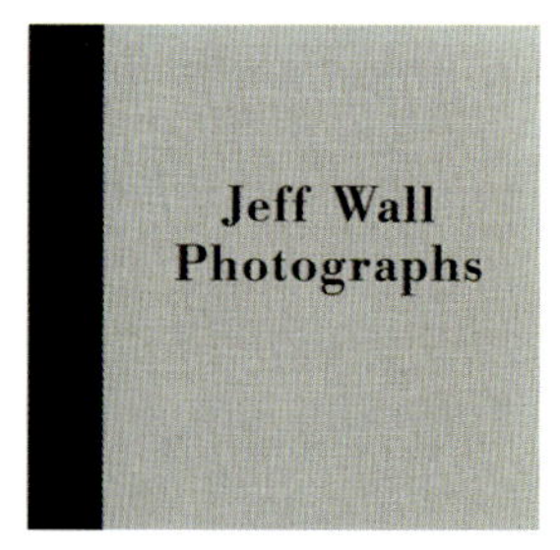

JEFF WALL: PHOTOGRAPHS
STEIDL/ HASSELBLAD CENTER

Clothbound & slipcased, 10.5 x 10.75 inches
156 pages / 28 color and 7 tritones
$50 ISBN 3-88243-867-3

EDITORS' NOTE

The given demand on the photographer is *to be there* (wherever *there* may be). The demand less easy to define or achieve is *to see*. And, as Henri Cartier-Bresson asserts in the following pages, "Seeing is questioning."

In this issue of *Aperture* we bring you questions, then, posed with regard to humanity, earthly beauty, and unrepressed spirit.

We have the extraordinary honor of including here a number of previously unpublished images by Cartier-Bresson, accompanied by an interview with the photographer, conducted by *Aperture*'s Editor at Large, Diana Stoll. Cartier-Bresson chose to publish these images on the occasion of a major retrospective of his work at the Bibliothèque Nationale in Paris, and the inauguration of the new HCB Foundation. *Aperture* is very grateful to Cartier-Bresson for agreeing to work with us, and to his wife, the wonderful photographer Martine Franck, to his agent Helen Wright, and to Magnum for facilitating this exciting opportunity.

Seeing is questioning. The year 1968 was a vital, definitive moment in the world's political history—and also represented an important time in society's relationship to photography. Now, thirty-five years later, we are again in a period of great conflict, protest, violence, and the ready potential for more violence. But, as Fred Ritchin points out in this issue, our affinity with photography has changed radically and irrevocably in the years since 1968. Ritchin recalls that seminal period, when cultural imperialism was challenged, when protest and dissent were assumed to be privileges inherent to democracy—and when images took an interrogatory role they may never again be able to play in the same way.

Photographer Larry Towell questions the conventional depiction of circumstances in Palestine, and offers his own sensitive, humane, and telling approach based on his long-term coverage of the area. Here, he shows a series of images from the Israeli-occupied territories, focusing on last year's conflict in Jenin, that go far beyond the ubiquitous sight-bite media coverage; Towell brings a human understanding to this "no man's land," and achieves a level of insight that only time and compassion can allow.

In another territory—another world—photographer Andrea Modica looks with a poetic, seductive eye at an unexpected wilderness: the lush patches of green that grow between the tracts, so to speak, in suburban and parkland Florida. Vince Aletti, who spent much of his childhood exploring the secret swamps and jungles of Fort Lauderdale, contributes an intimate narrative to accompany Modica's spellbinding, strangely surreal images. Aletti invokes the insuppressible wildness behind the beauty of these places.

Wildness is integral also to the classic Argentine art form: tango. Renowned writer, art historian, and cultural critic Robert Farris Thompson explores the roots and spirit of the dance, in an essay as lively and loving as tango itself. He writes of the dance's enduring "humanism": "Tango's strength and elegance outlast negation; the motion and the music defy life's brevity." Accompanying Thompson's essay are Argentinean photographer Adriana Groisman's sensuous, motion-filled images that capture the controlled fever of the dance.

Also in this issue, we commemorate the lives and work of two photographers, friends, and colleagues: Manuel Alvarez Bravo and Inge Morath. Their passing marks the closing of an extraordinary era for the medium of photography. We will miss them greatly.

Seeing is indeed questioning. And questioning—on the part of both photographer and audience—demands engagement and concern. Although our relationship to photography may well have been transformed over the past decades, we can hope that such close interrogation may still have the power to incite us to act, to move us to think for ourselves, and when necessary, to challenge and protest.

©2002 Nikon Inc.
Once-in-a-lifetime shots happen once. So when opportunity comes knocking, Nikon's Total Imaging System is ready to answer the door. Consider our 70-180mm AF Micro-Nikkor Zoom lens with Nikon ED glass for sharp, high-contrast images. It helps you get up close and personal with its 1:1.33 reproduction ratio. When it's teamed with our new digital cameras, like the D1x, details are revealed with extraordinary clarity.

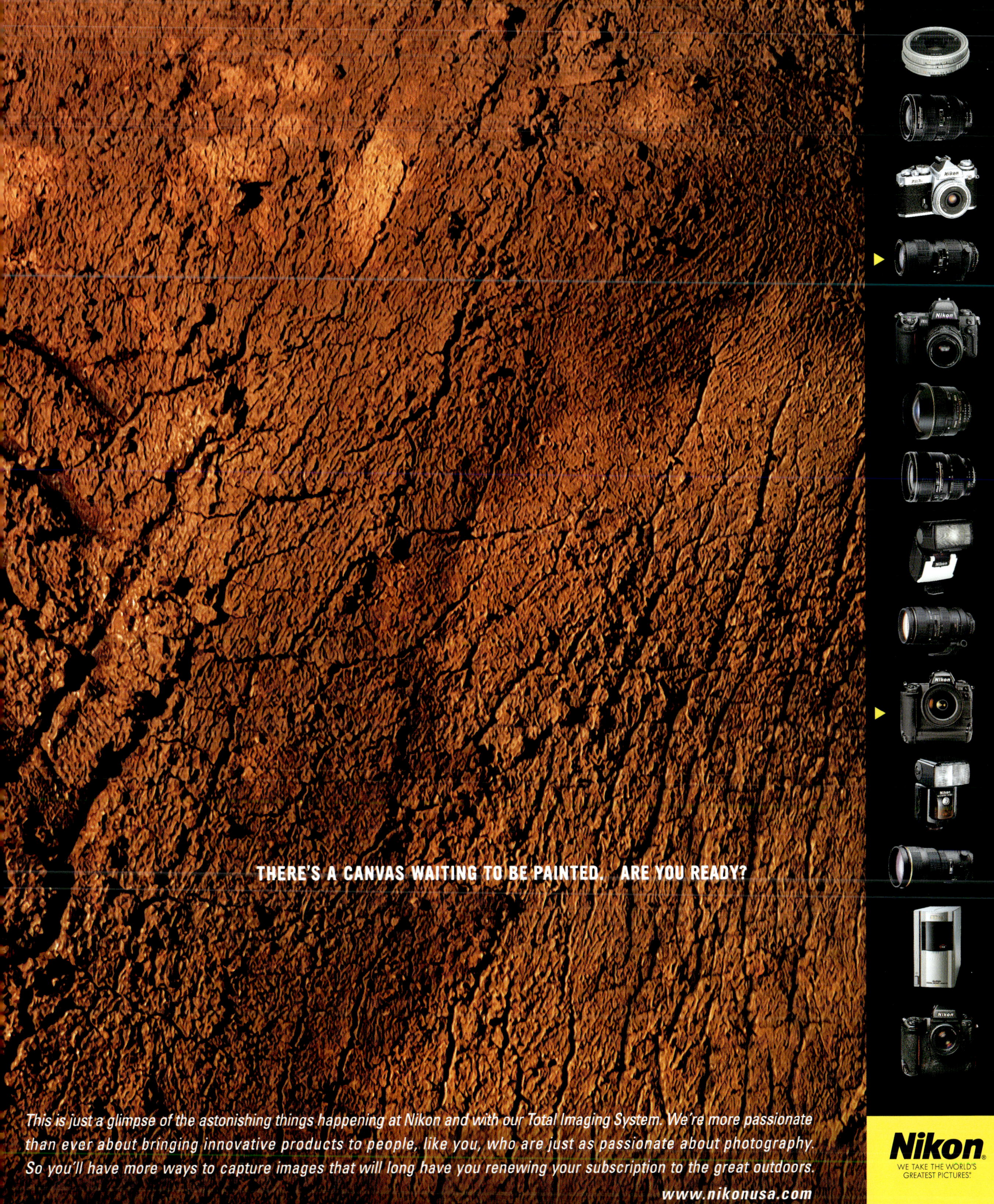
THERE'S A CANVAS WAITING TO BE PAINTED.   ARE YOU READY?

This is just a glimpse of the astonishing things happening at Nikon and with our Total Imaging System. We're more passionate
than ever about bringing innovative products to people, like you, who are just as passionate about photography.
So you'll have more ways to capture images that will long have you renewing your subscription to the great outdoors.

www.nikonusa.com

Nikon
WE TAKE THE WORLD'S
GREATEST PICTURES.

MOVING PICTURES

BY ROSELEE GOLDBERG

How did photography and "moving pictures" come to take center stage of the art world at the turn of the new century? Why are museums and galleries of contemporary art from New York to Tokyo to Johannesburg today filled with large-scale, spectacular photographs and high-definition video projections? The Guggenheim Museum's "Moving Pictures," with more than 150 works by fifty-five contemporary artists working in photography, film, and video, goes far in advancing an explanation for this development in the visual arts.

Whether museum visitors view this exhibition forward or backward in chronological order—depending on whether one starts at the bottom of the Guggeheim's famous curved ramp, with Nam June Paik's *TV Garden* (1974) or from the top with Bill Viola's *Going Forth By Day* (2002)— "Moving Pictures" offers an exciting and informative journey through almost four decades of art and cultural history.

The fact that this story is told using works from the Guggenheim's permanent collection, including the museum's acquisitions and gifts from notable collectors and foundations, raises another question: *how* do such institutions keep track of contemporary history as it is being made? While collections have much to do with visionary curators, the availability of desirable artworks, the right price, and the generosity of benefactors, they must, at best, establish a ground plan for understanding a particular period, while at the same time allowing for future expansion and revision.

"Moving Pictures" is a fine example of these many factors at work. The show's emphasis on the photograph as an artistic vehicle is clear, and its coverage of large-scale portraiture and architectural interiors, as well as film installations by international artists, is especially strong. Inevitably, these factors may also account for some notable absences of artists whose work is important to this evolving history: John Baldessari, Louise Lawler, and Dan Graham, for example, as well as the very influential early works of Cindy Sherman.

This collection begins its trajectory in the late 1960s and early 1970s, with works by Vito Acconci, Marina Abramovic, Bruce Nauman, and Ana Mendieta, artists who are described in the museum's wall notes and brochure as "employing photographic strategies." In fact, these people were using the camera in ways that were anathema to the trained photographer; the process of

Sam Taylor Wood, *Soliloquy III*, 1998.

lighting, framing, developing, and printing each photograph on particular paper in a particular format and size integral to the aesthetic and originality of the photographer's art was of no interest to these visual artists. Their focus, rather, was on art's underlying intellectual premises and perception-altering possibilities. They investigated these possibilities through private and public performances that they photographed themselves or had photographed, by artist-friends or straight documentarians. These images, deliberately deprived of any qualities that might call attention to them as finished artworks, were always understood as "documentation," never as photographs. And it was this approach that char-

acterized the work of a generation of conceptual artists, including Christian Boltanski, Sophie Calle, and Annette Messager, whose photographs originated in live activities.

These artists mostly used "performance-art strategies" rather than photographic ones to construct their images. Sherman certainly did. Tutored in camera basics, she paid little attention to developing or printing her material; her early photographs were processed commercially in standard sizes and then thumbtacked to gallery walls. It was concept, not product, that drove Sherman, whose *Untitled Film Stills* were pivotal in altering forever the marketplace of the photograph in the visual-arts world. (Robert Mapplethorpe once bemoaned the fact that, because he was a photographer, his prices would never match hers). Indeed, Sherman is certainly one of the most influential artists of the final decades of the twentieth century, and it is her groundbreaking early work, as a visual artist with camera in hand, that gave so many artists in this exhibition (including Janine Antonini, Vanessa Beecroft, Anna

LEFT, TOP: Candida Höfer, *Deichmanske Bibliothek Oslo* II, 2000; LEFT, BOTTOM: Rineke Dijkstra, *Coney Island, New York, USA, July 9, 1993*; RIGHT: Bernd and Hilla Becher, *Wassertürme* (Water towers), 1980.

Gaskell, and Matthew Barney) license to proceed.

In Europe in the 1970s, Bernd and Hilla Becher's black-and-white photographs of industrial buildings exemplified the anti-aesthetic creed of conceptual art. No hint at romance or emotion was evoked by the deteriorating nineteenth-century structures they placed front and center in their photographs. The Bechers' vast anthology of architectural silhouettes has a sparse and detached sensibility—no clouds, no landscape, no horizon-line intrude on their images—which was achieved by shooting on overcast days only. Students of the Bechers

who have become well known in their own right—Andreas Gursky, Candida Höfer, Thomas Ruff, and Thomas Struth among them—inherited their instructors' purist methods of isolating and serially recording a chosen subject. Each, however, added brilliant color, digital processing, and—of enormous consequence—grand scale. Closer in size to salon paintings of earlier periods, the works of these artists (like that of Dutch artist Rineke Dijkstra, among others) comprise a new school of visual art photography that further emphasizes the art historical awareness behind this work. Formal properties

WWW.PAULSMITH.CO.UK
PAUL
SMITH
PULL
Paul Smith

of composition and color, as well as the conceptual devices that mark the style and content of each artist's oeuvre are evidence of a continuing evolution of the debates regarding image, landscape, and the body that were initiated by conceptual artists in the 1970s.

Another stimulus for "big picture" photographs has been the seduction of the big screen. Whether enthralled by directors Alfred Hitchcock or Stephen Spielberg, Sidney Lumet or Andy Warhol, artists from Sam Taylor Wood to Gregory Crewdson, Stan Douglas to Pierre Huyghe have all used cinematic strategies to create photographs and film projections in a visual-art context. As with the nuanced distinctions between photography and the photographs of visual artists, so too these artists consciously isolate aspects of film for their own purposes; they examine not only how the viewer sees, but also how the viewer feels and comprehends while in the process of viewing film.

Shirin Neshat's film installations purposefully exploit the gallery space as a more experiential place than the movie theater, where the viewer's sensual connection to the image can be measured. For Neshat, the starting point is "the image, and nothing else," she says.

Like William Kentridge, Neshat focuses on raw politics and its impact on individual lives. Indeed, the way Kentridge makes his animations seems to be in direct response to the brutalization of humanity in the police state that was apartheid-era South Africa. His act of drawing and erasing, which he uses to construct his animated films, probably has more to do with his emotional needs than with an interest in developing a particular animation technique.

LEFT: Marina Abramovic, *Rhythm 5*, **1974;**
ABOVE: Gregory Crewdson, *Untitled (Pregnant woman-pool)*, **1999.**

"Moving Pictures" demands hours of viewing; not just because several of the projected works run for many minutes, but also because it is a vast collection of material that needs to be understood within numerous overlapping histories. Fortunately, it was on view for more than six months, although such a collection, describing the evolution of media-related material of the past forty years, truly deserves a space for permanent viewing. ◐

"Moving Pictures" was presented at New York's Guggenheim Museum, June 28, 2002– January 12, 2003.

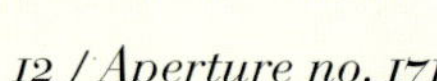

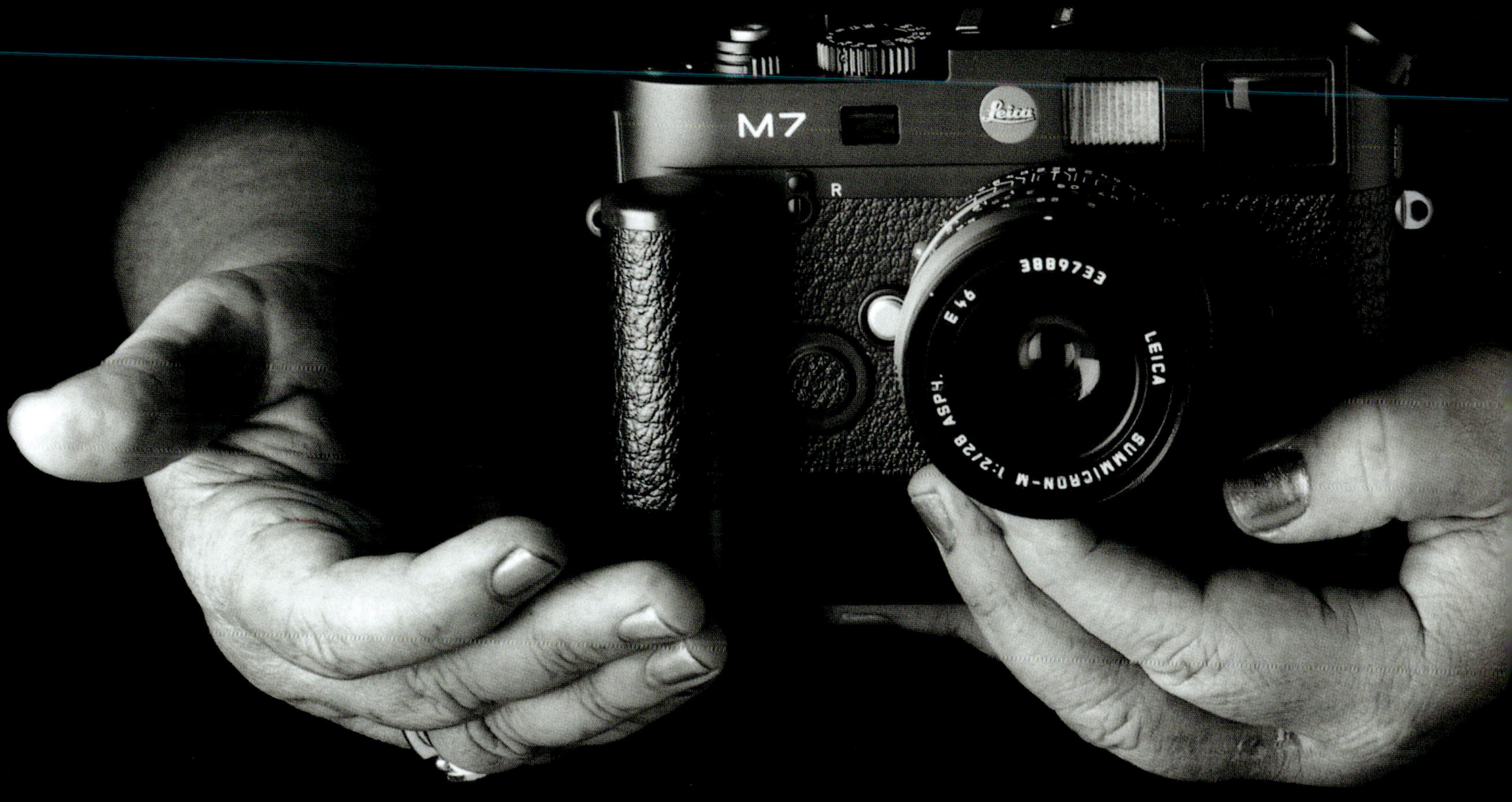
M7
R
3889733
E46
LEICA
SUMMICRON-M 1:2/28 ASPH.

IMAGES FROM NO MAN'S LA

APERTURE

May, 2003

Dear Reader,

I want to take this opportunity to introduce myself to you. On January 22, I assumed the position of Executive Director of the Aperture Foundation, which includes this magazine, Aperture books, limited-edition prints, and traveling exhibitions.

It is a great honor to be associated with such a groundbreaking organization. My own background has been primarily in art criticism, exhibitions, and museum management; my focus until some ten years ago was therefore primarily on painting and sculpture, especially contemporary. I was a deputy director of the Museum of Modern Art when I was offered the directorship of the Montclair Art Museum, a post I held for 8½ years. Soon after arriving at MAM, I began to acquire photography for their collection of more than 15,000 examples of American art. Within a very short time, I was hooked. I had discovered what you already know—that photographs provide an incomparable window into history, material culture, and private obsessions and that photography today is practiced or borrowed by all kinds of artists, often with strikingly original results.

Aperture magazine was launched fifty years ago to provide a means for fine art photographers in the United States to communicate with each other. Over the years, collectors and photography lovers have joined their ranks; our subscribers—and subject matter—are dispersed throughout the globe. It is my intention to help Aperture serve the photographic community in the twenty-first century by consistently and fearlessly:

- reevaluating the history of photography as a medium.
- bringing new perspective to past masters.
- providing insight into the work of living masters.
- introducing younger artists who are innovative or who, in our opinion, are "just" making beautiful, significant photographs or photo-based artwork.

If you have suggestions about how we can accomplish all of these goals more effectively, or if you have thoughts about the goals themselves, I hope you will consider sending me an e-mail at director@aperture.org.

Thank you for your ongoing support of photography and the Aperture Foundation. I look forward to serving you in the years ahead.

Yours sincerely,

Ellen S. Harris
Executive Director

20 EAST 23RD STREET, NEW YORK, NEW YORK 10010-4463 TEL (212)505-5555 / FAX (212)979-7759

WWW.APERTURE.ORG

The following is an excerpt from the Human Rights Watch report titled "Jenin: IDF (Israeli Defence Forces) Military Operations."

On April 3, 2002, the Israeli Defense Forces (IDF) launched a major military operation in the Jenin refugee camp, home to some fourteen thousand Palestinians, the overwhelming major-ity of them civilians. The Israelis' expressed aim was to capture or kill Palestinian militants responsible for suicide bombings and other attacks that have killed more than seventy Israeli and other civilians since March 2002. The IDF military incursion into the Jenin refugee camp was carried out on an unprecedented scale compared to other military operations mounted by the IDF since the current Israeli-Palestinian conflict began in September 2000.

The presence of armed Palestinian militants inside Jenin refugee camp, and the preparations made by those armed Palestinian militants in anticipation of the IDF incursion, does not detract from the IDF's obligation under international humanitarian law to take all feasible precautions to avoid harm to civilians. Israel also has a legal duty to ensure that

ND LARRY TOWELL IN JENIN

its attacks on legitimate military targets did not cause disproportionate harm to civilians. Unfortunately, these obligations were not met. Human Rights Watch's research demonstrates that, during their incursion into the Jenin refugee camp, Israeli forces committed serious violations of international humanitarian law, some amounting *prima facie* to war crimes.

Due to the dense urban setting of the refugee camp, fighters and civilians were never at great distances. Civilian residents of the camp described days of sustained missile fire from helicopters hitting their houses. Some residents were forced to flee from house to house seeking shelter, while others were trapped by the fighting, unable to escape to safety, and were threatened by a curfew that the IDF enforced with lethal force, using sniper fire. Human Rights Watch documented instances in which soldiers converted civilian houses into military positions, and confined the inhabitants to a single room. In other instances, civilians who attempted to flee were expressly told by IDF soldiers that they should return to their homes.

. . . The IDF used armored bulldozers to demolish residents' homes. The apparent purpose was to clear paths through Jenin's narrow and winding alleys to enable their tanks and other heavy weaponry to penetrate the camp interior, particularly since some of these had evidently been booby-trapped. However, particularly in the Hawashin district, the destruction extended well beyond any conceivable purpose of gaining access to fighters, and was vastly disproportionate to the military objectives pursued. The damage to Jenin camp by missile and tank fire and bulldozer has shocked many observers. At least 140 buildings—most of them multifamily dwellings—were completely destroyed in the camp, and severe damage caused to more than two hundred others has rendered them uninhabitable or unsafe. An estimated four thousand people, more than a quarter of the population, were rendered homeless because of this destruc-

tion. Serious damage has been done to the water, sewage, and electrical infrastructure of the camp.

Human Rights Watch has confirmed that at least fifty-two Palestinians were killed as a result of IDF operations in Jenin. . . . At least twenty-two of those confirmed dead were civilians, including children, physically disabled, and elderly people. At least twenty-seven of those confirmed dead were suspected to have been armed Palestinians belonging to movements such as Islamic Jihad, Hamas, and the al-Aqsa Martyr's Brigade. Some were members of the Palestinian Authority's (PA) National Security Forces or other branches of the PA police and security forces.

Human Rights Watch found no evidence to sustain claims of massacres or large-scale extrajudicial executions by the IDF in Jenin refugee camp. However, many of the civilian deaths documented by HRW amounted to unlawful or willful killings by the IDF. Many others could have been avoided if the IDF had taken proper precautions to protect civilian life during its military operation, as required by international humanitarian law.

Among the civilian deaths were those of Kamal Zgheir, a fifty-seven-year-old wheelchair-bound man who was shot and run over by a tank on a major road outside the camp on April 10, even though he had a white flag attached to his wheelchair; fifty-eight-year-old Mariam Wishahi, killed by a missile in her home on April 6 just hours after her unarmed son was shot in the street; Jamal Fayid, a thirty-seven-year-old paralyzed man who was crushed in the rubble of his home on April 7 despite his family's pleas to be allowed to remove him; and fourteen-year-old Faris Zaiban, who was killed by fire from an IDF armored car as he went to buy groceries when the IDF-imposed curfew was temporarily lifted on April 11.

. . . Throughout the incursion, IDF soldiers used Palestinian civilians to protect them from danger, deploying them as "human shields" and forcing them to perform dangerous work. HRW received many separate and credible testimonies that Palestinians were placed in vulnerable positions to protect IDF soldiers from gunfire or attack. IDF soldiers forced these Palestinians to stand for extended periods in front of exposed

IDF positions, or made them accompany the soldiers as they moved from house to house.

. . . HRW has so far found no evidence that Palestinian gunmen forced Palestinian civilians to serve as human shields during the attack. But Palestinian gunmen did endanger Palestinian civilians in the camp by using it as a base for planning and launching attacks, using indiscriminate tactics such as planting improvised explosive devices within the camp, and intermingling with the civilian population during the armed conflict, and, in some cases, to avoid apprehension by Israeli forces.

. . . During the period that the IDF directly controlled Jenin camp, the Israeli authorities were obliged under international humanitarian law to take all feasible precautions to protect camp civilians . . . and ensure to the maximum extent possible under the circumstances that the civilian population had access to food and medical supplies. In practice, however, the IDF prevented humanitarian organizations, including the International Committee of the Red Cross, from gaining access to the camp and its civilian inhabitants—despite the great humanitarian need. ◐

*I started screaming, asking anyone to call
an ambulance. The ambulance came, but it was prevented
from reaching us. Atiya was still breathing
at the time. But there was no aid, no ambulance.
I couldn't go outside because there were Israeli snipers
and tanks everywhere. All this time we were just
crawling. After all my trials trying to get anyone to help,
I went back to the body. I started checking,
and made sure he died. I closed his eyes and straightened his
hands. I closed the door because I didn't want
my children to see their father dead. He had promised
to buy the children some milk before he died,
and they kept asking where the milk was. . . . I spent the
whole night with the children in one room.
I couldn't close my eyes. At midnight, I went to
the room and put a blanket over him.*

—Human Rights Watch interview with
Hala' Muhammad Abu Rumaila, age thirty-one,
Jenin, April 21, 2002

*We were inside in a room and saw some smoke.
The soldiers were asking us to open the door.
My sister 'Afaf went to the door to open it, and while she
was opening it, the bomb exploded. When the bomb exploded,
we were all screaming, calling for an
ambulance. The soldiers were laughing. We saw the right
side of her face was destroyed, and the left
side of her shoulder and arm was also wounded.
She was killed that first moment.*

—Human Rights Watch interview with
Aisha 'Ali Disuqi, age thirty-seven, Jenin, April 19, 2002

*I was in the first floor apartment. When the
missile hit, we felt it, and we came to the third floor and
saw the missile there [it had come through the ceiling]
and we knew that Yusra must be dead. I came upstairs,
to try to be sure, but we couldn't come in because
the helicopters were still in the sky, so we went back
downstairs. The fifth day of the attack,
soldiers occupied the first three floors of the building,
we asked to come take her body, to send it to the hospital,
but they refused to let us.*

—Human Rights Watch interview with
Abdul-Karim Ahmad Mohmad Khorj, age thirty-one,
Jenin, April 27, 2002

Notes from NO MAN'S LAND

X

Occupied East Jerusalem,
November 17, 2001

In the Arab Quarter tonight
I asked for Lion's Gate.
A blind man overheard.
"Follow me," he said.
He knew his way by touch
tapping through darkness,
the shadows of other men.
A glass window
burst into flame
as the sun hit it.
"Calm down. Calm down,"
he said to the sun.
He'd felt the heat on his face.
The sun was gone by the time I passed.
The sound his cane made on stones
scared a bird from its balcony.
"Calm down," he said to the bird.
He tapped on a stone ten times
& the bird came back.
He turned around
to feel the wind on his eyes
asking, "How far away is the sky?"
Then I heard church bells
clap heavy brass tongues.
"Must be Sunday," he said.
"Bells ring every day in Jerusalem,"
I replied. He shook his head.
He was listening to bells
in far-off towns.
Then a cat jumped
one roof to the next
frightened by the bells. "Calm down,"
he said to the cat.
It peeked over the edge

as the man passed by.
"How far away is the sky?" he asked again.
The evening walk was over
when we reached Lion's Gate.
Policemen tapped stone walls
with night sticks.
I heard a soft click.
A machine gun's safety catch slid
back & forth.
"It's above your head," he said.
I looked up at the silhouette of a soldier
leaning into the moon
as if dreaming of romance
somewhere else.
"Calm down," he said.
& the soldier stopped
to peer over the edge.
I didn't know if the gun was on or off.
"Don't worry," he said,
"It's off."
The soldier leaned back into position
like a sniper waiting
for someone among the crickets
to move.
A star fell over the wall
& dropped into the crickets.
I said, "You knew where the bird was
& the proximity of the sun.
The cat & the soldier
both heard you.
You asked about the sky.
The sky is all around them."

"It's about killing," he said.

"How far away
did you say the star was?"

—Larry Towell

In the charred remains of homes household effects had been burned or melted right off the walls. Curtains, picture frames, rugs, bookshelves, even the electrical covers of light switches were vaporized. Some rooms bore ghostly smudges from human beings in the smoke.

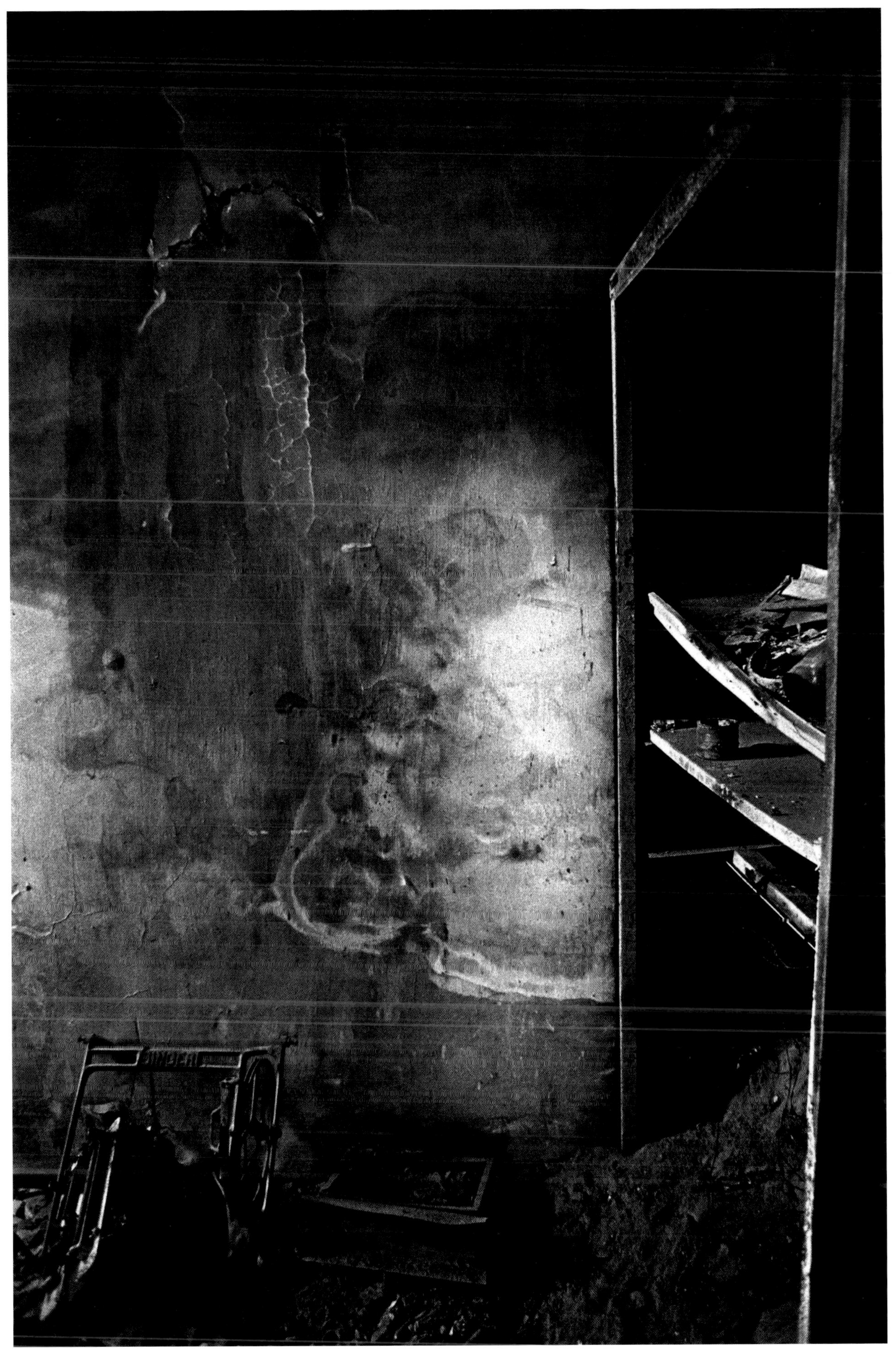

مخيم الموت
مخيم الاستشهاد
مخيم العمود

wild thing

Andrea Modica's Florida Landscapes

by Vince Aletti

We moved to Florida—my mother, my two younger sisters, and I—after my father had been killed in a small-plane crash. I was eleven and didn't understand why my mother could no longer bear the suburban Philadelphia house we lived in, the house I never wanted to leave. So I hated Florida, but loved the swamps. At least I thought of them as swamps: the overgrown empty lots bordering two sides of the property that held our four-unit motel. There were frogs there and when it rained—which was nearly every afternoon in a brief, tropical downpour—the lots filled ankle-deep or deeper and tadpoles swarmed. The water soaked into the sandy soil quickly most days, leaving a lacy brown scum between the reeds. No one came to mow the wild grasses or to cut the weeds in the lots, but we flattened them for paths, our sandals making sucking sounds in the mud. We chased fireflies there, and snatched at the butterflies drifting over the wildflowers. We pretended to be lost in the jungle. And we disappeared into its tangle of green to play with dolls and toy soldiers under a canopy of wide-bladed grass.

Fort Lauderdale in the mid fifties was a boomtown in slow motion, far from its former wilderness but still sleepy and not yet overbuilt. One end of our street broke off abruptly at the edge of a wooded tract full of dark pines and seagrape. The people who lived there kept monkeys that often escaped to entertain patrons at a hotel bar nearby. Alligators sometimes crawled out of the canals into people's landscaped backyards. Small green lizards darted across the sidewalks and hopped onto the lawn furniture, alert as birds, throats throbbing. Huge palm fronds, their tips gone brown and frayed into fine threads, littered the lawns. Mold blossomed between the pages of books and along the seams of faded pink stucco walls. The dampness, the bugs, the clinging vines, the sudden storms, the heat: even when nothing was happening, there was the oddly satisfying sense that something was slipping out of control.

I guess I was, too. I deliberately missed the school bus or, once on board, burst into tears. I wanted to be alone in my room with my books, or in a vacant lot hidden among the reeds.

My world was small, miniaturized, taking up only a little space—the land at the base of a flower, the interior of a shoebox—but I claimed that space, ruled that space. I was imagining someplace private, secret—a place where I belonged—but I never imagined it was someplace safe. The land would flood or get trampled; the shoebox homes were always burned. I knew these things happened in life. I accepted fate, even hastened it: if natural forces didn't wipe out my dirt villages, I would destroy them anyway. I welcomed toy disasters. I was resilient; I could survive; I proved it over and over. I could lose something—something I took real pleasure in creating—and just pick up and start again.

But sometimes make-believe was all I was capable of. Even after I resigned myself to school, I was always in another world. Something was going on in my body that was baffling and embarrassing and thrilling, but it was also something that no one else could know about. Sex—the idea of sex, because I had never gotten any further than that—confused me utterly, but I couldn't forget about it even when I tried. Kids in school talked about it all the time; they seemed to know everything. But how? They weren't any older than the friends I'd left behind up North, who were just as ignorant as I was. Still, no amount of knowledge could have explained my dreams or the fantasies that seeped into more and more of my waking life, leaving me breathless, stunned. The less I understood what was happening to me, the more compelling it was. I was developing a taste for chaos.

Sun City, Florida, 1998.

So I loved the thunderstorms, the brief summer squalls with their drenching rain, the vagrant hurricanes whipping through offshore. I stood waist-deep in the undergrowth of the empty lots, excited by all that ripeness and rot, the sweet, green smell of things growing wild and going bad. I was probably reading too much Carson McCullers and Truman Capote, losing myself in some damaged dream of the South, in the romance of decay. But Florida, especially the tourist's Gold Coast, was hardly the Deep South. Even its recent history was paved over and meticulously landscaped. A third of the buildings in Fort Lauderdale had gone up in the decade before we arrived, and virtually all of them were inhabited by people like us, who had moved down from Up North. We hardly ever met anyone who had been born in Florida. What little real history the city had was already packaged for visitors. The Seminole village that was a featured stop on the *Jungle Queen* cruise through Lauderdale's network of waterways was a pathetic relic. The men wrestled alligators and the women sold cloth dolls and bright rickrack skirts out of palm-thatched huts no one ever lived in. It was a relief to get back to the fat yachts, swimming pools, and Spanish-style "mansions" that dotted the Intercoastal. Florida was not about the past; it was about starting over, making it big, and forgetting.

But the land has a memory, and Andrea Modica is tuned right into it. Her photographs of Florida landscapes might slam me back to childhood fantasyland, but they also remind me that what still

THIS PAGE: *Myakka, Florida*, 1998; OPPOSITE: *Aripeka, Florida*, 1998.

remains of the swamps—the forgotten tracts, the rutted dirt trails, the riot of green—hasn't lost its power to seduce and startle. Step out onto even the most manicured lawn and you sense the swamp is poised for a comeback. Abandoned lots turn into dense thicket overnight. The wasteland behind the mini-mall disappears under pine needles, marshgrass, and roots trailing across the muck. Strung with kudzu and broken branches, a patch of scrubland at the side of the road could be the entrance to a primordial jungle.

This is the territory Modica stakes out for her Florida landscapes: the wilderness next door. She made these velvety photogravures on forays into the state's central interior from the Tampa area, never straying too far from the highway. But you don't have to penetrate deep into the Everglades to discover Florida at its most primitive. Although she did visit some of the area's park preserves, Modica found equally timeless vistas just around the corner from the Pick 'N Pay. But, save for a gutted tire or a glimpse of dusty road, civilization has left no mark here. Trailing vines and tender branches sketch calligraphic mysteries across Modica's pictures; leaves evaporate into the sun's blaze or blot it out behind a choking maze. All this raw, creeping lushness is almost alarming, but Modica plunges in and draws our eye to an impossibly lovely squiggle of wood, a sublime wash of light, a mass of fronds as intricate as an etching. Nature, as voracious and unchecked as a tidal wave, doesn't sit still for a formal portrait. Modica is a rapt witness to both its frenzy and its delicacy; behind the beauty is a hungry, wild thing. ◉

MOVING WITH AN ARM AROUND LIFE

by Robert Farris Thompson

Notes

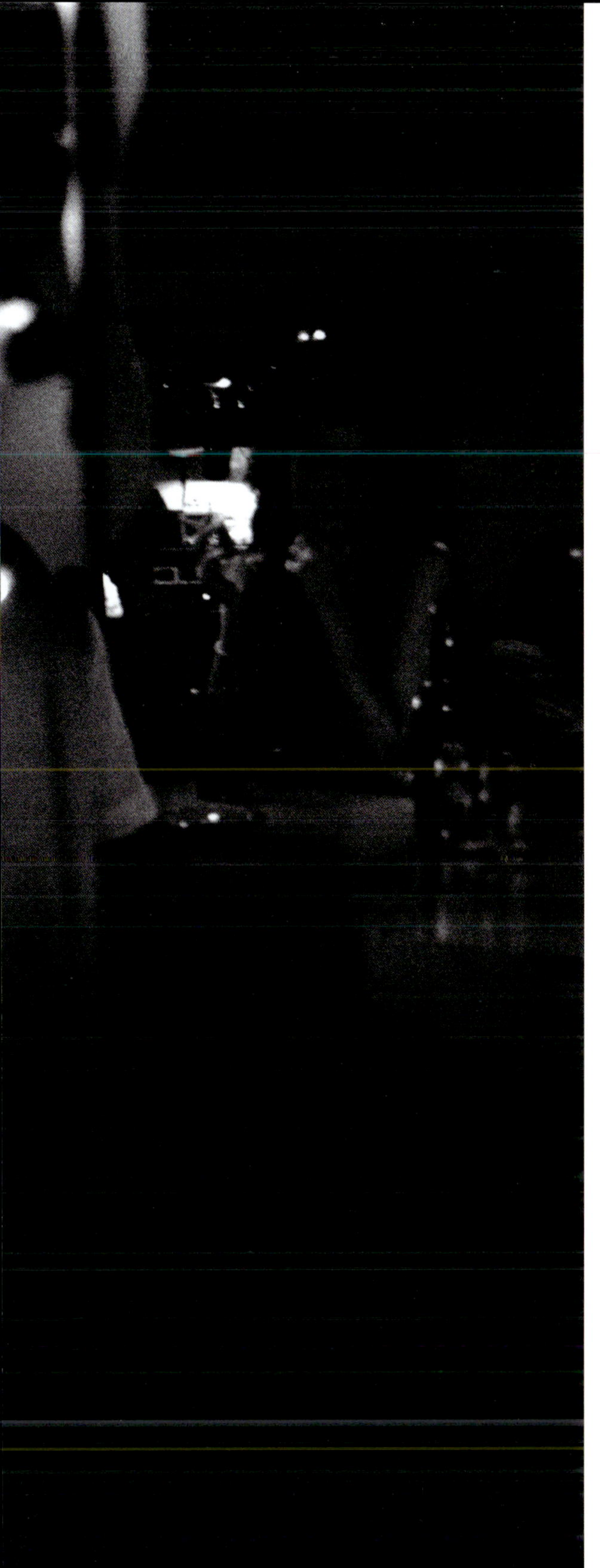

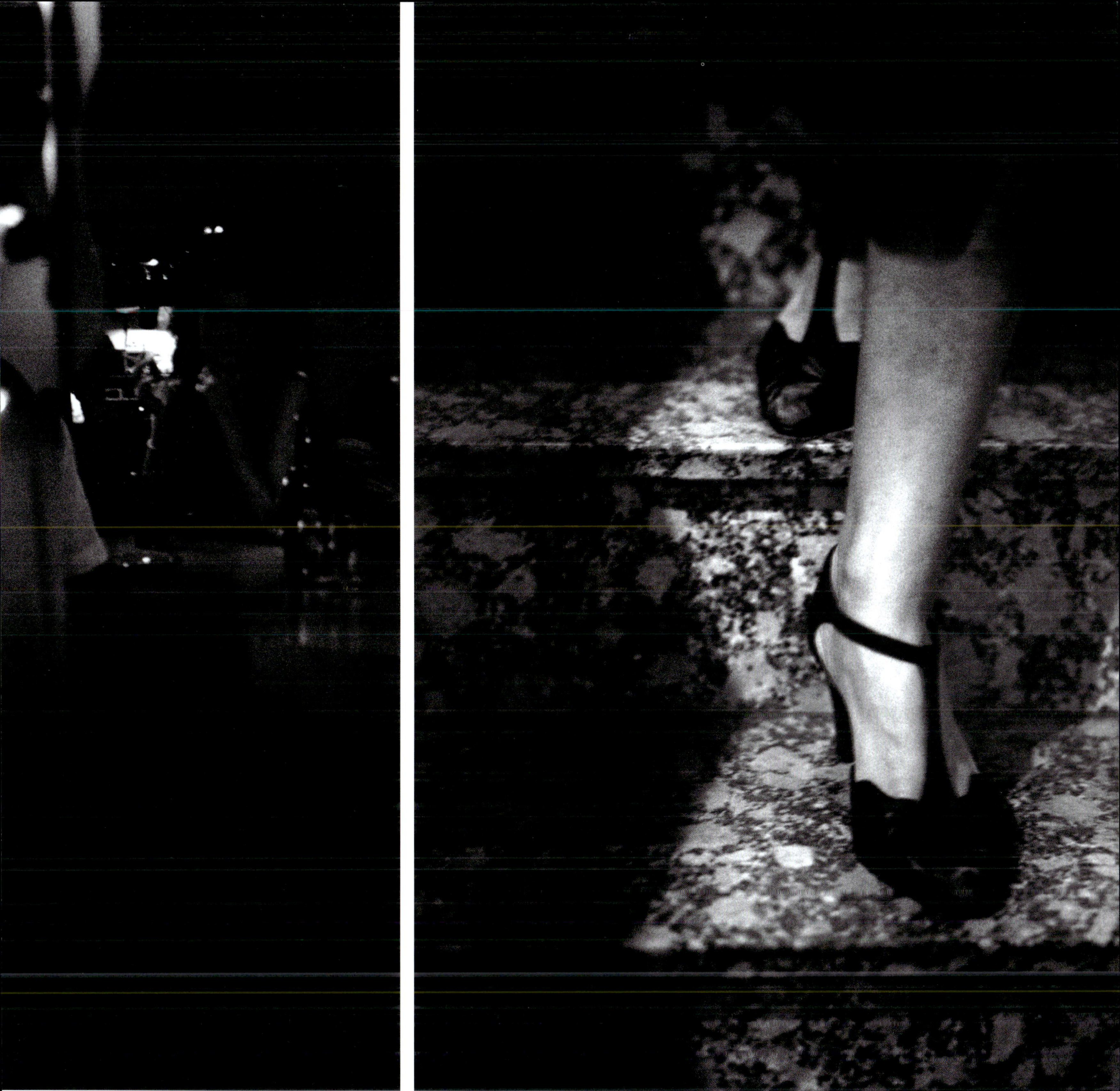

on Tango

Photographs by Adriana Groisman

—Jorge Luis Borges, *Antología personal*, 1961

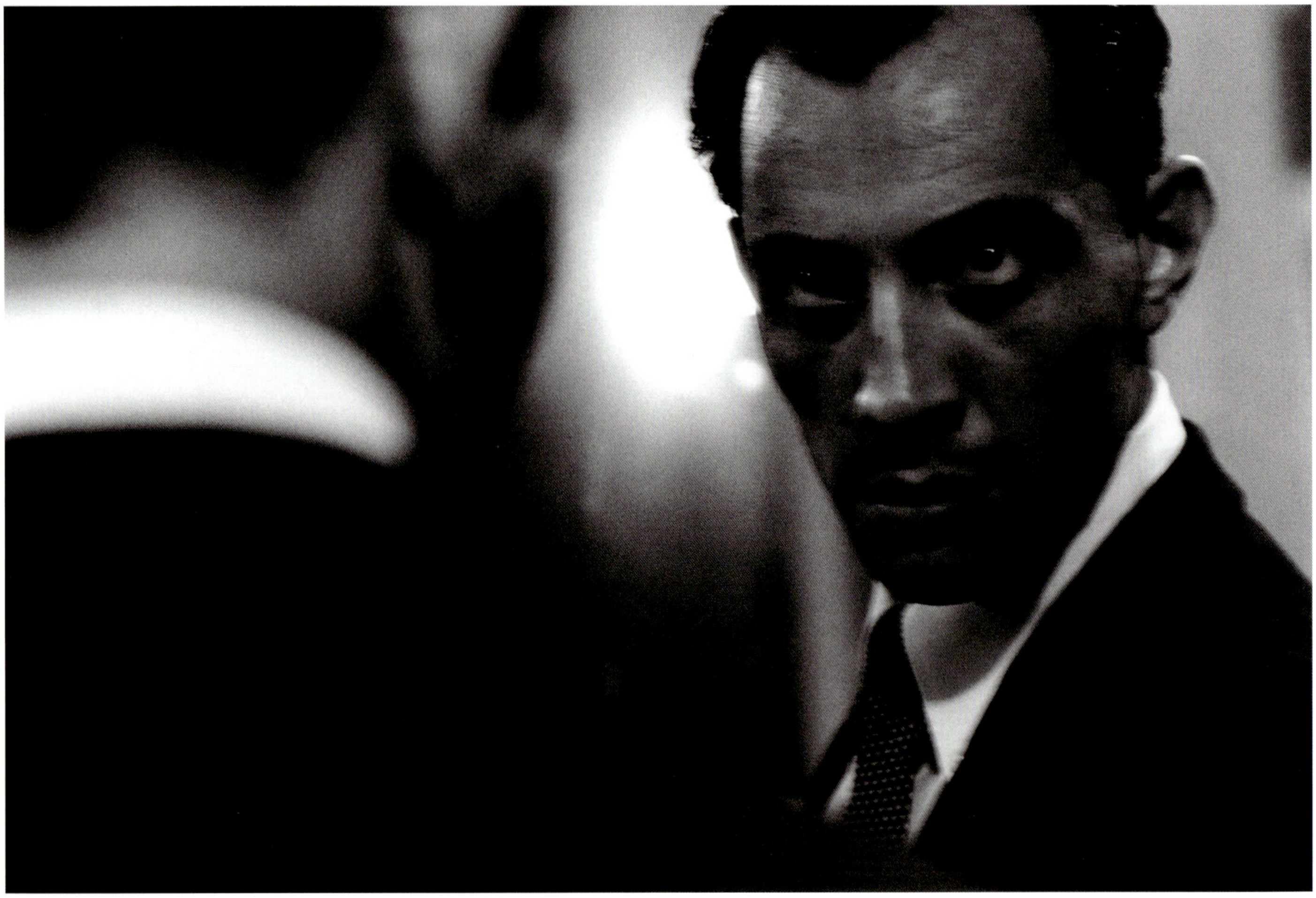

Tango is self-transformation.
—Sally Sommer, dance historian, 2000

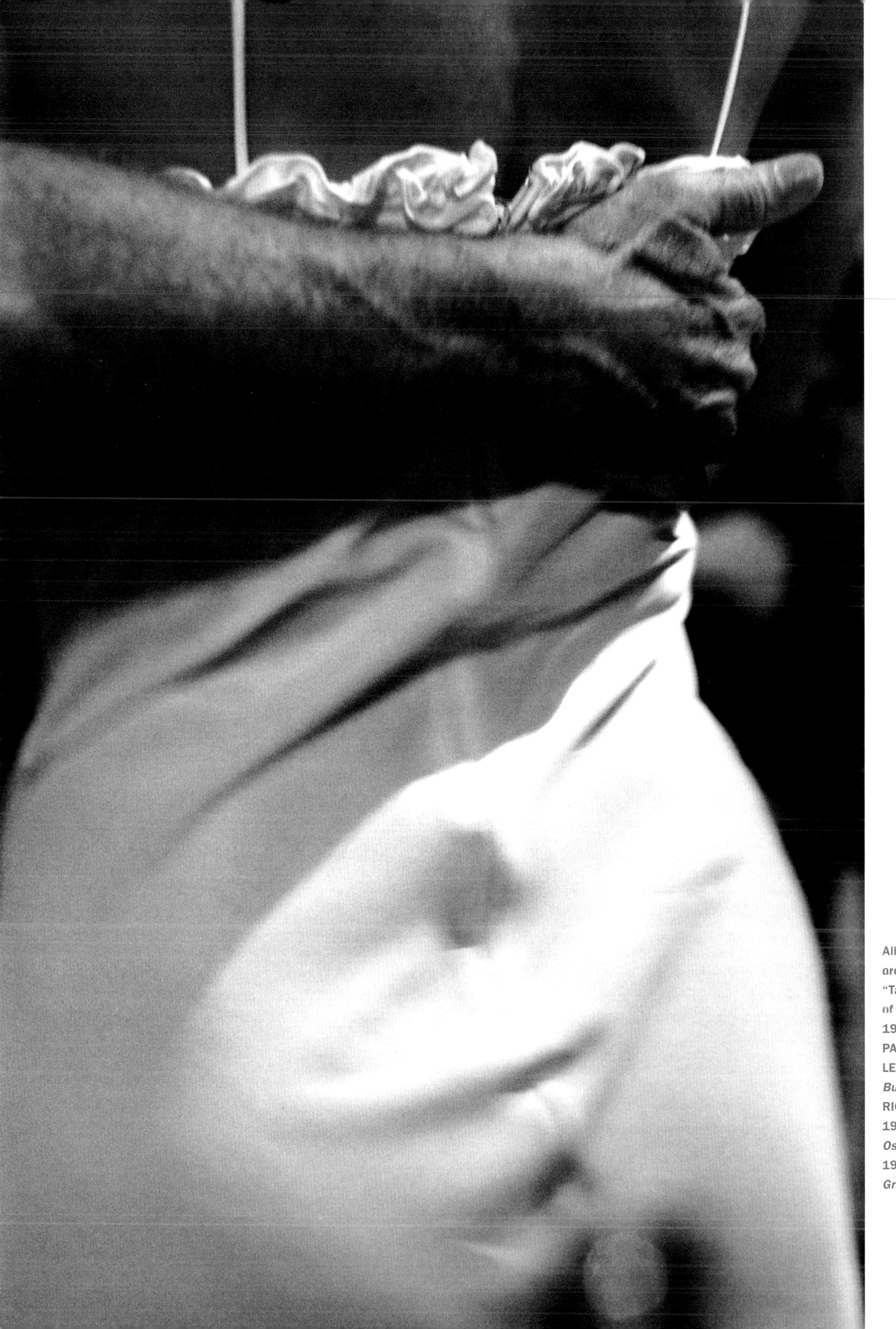

All photographs
are from the series
"Tango: The Dance
of the Night,"
1998–2000.
PAGES 34–35,
LEFT: *Regine,
Buenos Aires*, 1998;
RIGHT: *Glamour*,
1998; OPPOSITE:
Osvaldo at Home,
1998; THIS PAGE:
Gricel, 2000.

Tango spanned the twentieth century. It was *the* fabulous dance of the past hundred years—and the most beautiful, in the opinion of Martha Graham. Jorge Luis Borges divined one of the reasons for its staying power: tango translates outrage into music.

In 1934, in the depths of the Depression, Enrique Santos Discépolo wrote his classic tango lyric "Cambalache" (Shop where they sell stolen goods) for the film *The Soul of the Bandoneón*. "Cambalache" blasted its way into Argentine consciousness with words about time, immorality, and stoicism. Even today, *tangueros* know it cold: for them, it's the song that's never out of date.

In January 1999 I found a fragment from "Cambalache" graffitized on a Buenos Aires billboard, in the heart of the Barrio Norte:

> *20th century,*
> *feverish and problematic,*
> *[you're] a shop where they sell stolen goods*
> *You don't cry,*
> *you get no milk*
> *You don't cop it, you become a square*
> *But who the hell cares!*

Danger and violence confronted the world across the whole twentieth century. The women and men of tango kept going, turning outrage into song. The brave made abstractions of vicissitude. Small wonder that "Cambalache" became an anthem of *tangueros*, women and men who organize their lives around the music, and *milongueros*, women and men who organize their lives around the dance. Strong in stance, sure in motion, they gave the century a set of moves that spanned the globe and are with us forever.

Numerous books describe tango, the best evoking the passion of the form. Some are nostalgic, freezing time around the early twentieth century, the era of the *compadritos*, "tango hipsters," with their hats and cravats, their Victrolas with wide flaring horns, their kisses on street corners under a lamplight or the moon. Who cares that we're now in the twenty-first century? Tango is timeless, mixing love and action in the motion of the people. In the words of dancer Rodolfo Dinzel: "Tango has its own melody, movement, dance, literature, poetry, and argot—so we approach it as a classical tradition." Tango's strength and elegance outlast negation; the motion and the music defy life's brevity.

In the 1980s, Buenos Aires barrio dancers sparked the liveliest tango renaissance of the twentieth century through their performance in the stage extravaganza *Tango Argentino*. It had also been barrio dancers, led by the master Petróleo, who had sparked the earlier resurgence of the 1940s. Today the dance lives on, on the floors of the *milongas* (tango dance halls) of Buenos Aires. There, night after night, milongueros reveal why tango lasts: style conquers all.

The best tango narratives are strong, imparting truths and convictions. One basic message is: it is just as important to be well danced as it is to be well versed or well read. Tango's classic band leaders are larger than life: Roberto Firpo, Francisco Canaro, Julio de Caro, Carlos di Sarli, Juan D'Arienzo, Osvaldo Pugliese, Horacio Salgán, Anibal "Pichuco" Troilo, and Astor Piazzolla. More than music is involved: each master has written his own signature sound, demanding moves that are equally singular. Dancers like the late Lampazo or Roberto "El Alemán" Tonet translated D'Arienzo's virile rhythm into powerful, vivid figures. Di Sarli's sonic parsimony, by contrast, led to elegant refinement, in relatively few figures. Juan Carlos Copes could dance all of the above, and also to the jazz-inflected, classically tinged "new tango" of Piazzolla, itself built on the early modernism of the great tango pianists Salgán and Pugliese.

The inventor of the tango song was Carlos Gardel—he provided a Cheshire cat smile that lives even now in the air of Buenos Aires. The songs create moods of humor, valor, and longing, only the last of which overlaps a stereotype of tango as a song of anguish. Above all, tango poets make us aware of the passing of time. They *live* this awareness, which may be, *au fond*, the very essence of human consciousness.

In a piece on tango in the *New York Times*, Janny Scott observed that "followers" (a euphemism for females) were told not to move until the "leaders" indicated it was time. But she also discovered that tango women do not necessarily mirror what men are doing: "They often do different steps." How to comprehend the contradiction? Study the figures. In the *ocho*, a figure-eight pattern with mirroring pivots, the woman moves back and forth in a sinuous sequence that is wholly her own. At its best, the ocho becomes a bouquet of motion, tossed like eight roses at the feet of the partner. Ocho is a womanist original, set in motion by men.

La Ideal, 2000.

Women were singing tango before Gardel. The voices of Linda Thelma, Andrée Viviane, and Flora Gobbi are present on the earliest recorded tangos, from the first decade of the twentieth century. Their work leads on to the incredible Ada Falcón, "the Garbo of tango"; to Eladia Blásquez; and, finally to today's cantantes, such as Susana Rinaldi, Adriana Varela, Amelita Baltar, Lidia Borda, and Maria Cieri. In a macho country, to be a tango songstress was one of the ways a woman could "defend herself from hunger, the asphalt jungle—and men."

African and Afro-Argentine influences are continuous in the rise, development, and achievement of tango. As soon as one starts digging into the origins of the tango, its black Creole roots emerge. Even though Afro-Argentines had shrunk to a mere two thousand by the mid twentieth century, they were creating moves and composing tunes out of proportion to their numbers. Afro-

Argentines have been working at the center of tango from its earliest years right up to now.

The fact that celebrated black milongueros such as Carlos "El Negro" Anzuate, Margarita "La Negra" Grillé, and Facundo and Kely Posadas are equally conversant in jazz dance and in tango points to the fact that African influence is various. As Ricardo Rodríguez Molas notes, black impact on tango entails more than a single line of influence; the sources are multiple, and sometimes indirect. The beat of the Afro-Cuban habanera came to Argentina around 1850. This later led to the integration of key solo moves from the African-derived *candombe* dance in milonga couple-dancing in the Buenos Aires of the early and mid twentieth century. In addition, there were blacks who danced cakewalk and jazz in early twentieth-century Buenos Aires, as documented by Sergio Pujol. Finally, along with that triple black dosage—candombe, habanera, and

Today tango lives on, on the floors of the milongas of Buenos Aires. There,

La Estrella, 2000.

jazz—there came North African–influenced qualities too: Andalusian syncopation and percussive heel-stamping (*taconeo*) that trace back to the Moorish era in Spain surface briefly among tango masters like Copes.

Tango culture and tango humanism are Buenos Aires phenomena. They emerged from the encounter of dance concepts from the Kongo civilization of Africa with the city's complex cultural and social situation, involving Africa-born blacks, Argentina-born blacks, European migrants from Spain and Italy come to *hacer la America* (seek their fortune in the Americas), and Argentina-born Europeans, including ex-cattlemen, in from the pampas looking for work. The habanera rhythm arrived, in part, with black Cuban sailors, some settling on the other side of the Rio de la Plata in Montevideo, Uruguay, in the late nineteenth century. Habanera proved critical to the dance history of both Montevideo and Buenos Aires, where it provided the

Eventually young black dancers, and the whites and mulattoes who copied them, achieved the culturally impossible when they put together the early tango move *canyengue* (from the imperative of a Ki-Kongo verb *kanienge*, "be liquefied by heat"—i.e., melt into the music). This was a combination of "position one" in the classic dance of Central Africa—feet flat on the ground, bottom out, torso bent forward, face frozen—with the cheek-to-cheek, arms-around-the-partner romanticism of European embrace dancing. "Canyengue" became the name not only of a step but of a mode of being on the dance floor; elements of it live on in tango. Still danced by a coterie of special experts, canyengue reconnects us to the past. It gives us a measure for establishing the innovations in the subsequent forms of the dance. The name "canyengue" perfectly fits the dissolution of two styles into one. *Melting*, obviously, means getting hot, as when, in Kongo, an elder cries out "*Twisa ndungu!*" ("Put hot

beat of the milonga and of the earliest tangos.

All of these elements came together in late nineteenth-century Buenos Aires. But tango's strongest root is pure Afro-Argentine, a development of the Kongo-style dance elaborated in black dancing groups called *candombes*, which also existed in black Uruguay. Candombe steps were inserted into the habanera and the result was the milonga.

The habanera was originally a Kongo rhythm, a "call to the dance" (*mbila a makinu*) that in fusing with Iberian and other elements in Cuba took on a life of its own. The global diffusion of the habanera is amazing. It came to Argentina in the mid nineteenth century through no fewer than three sources: Spaniards who had danced it in Madrid, imported sheet music, and the black Cuban sailors who settled in Montevideo. A transnational phenomenon around 1850, habanera invaded the bars and dives and brothels of Buenos Aires and Montevideo. It challenged local black dancers and their comrades, sparking competitive invention among the barrio dancers, who were culturally prepared to receive and vary the basic Afro-Cuban beat. They looked for style. They played with rhythm. They flaunted newness. When the smoke cleared, the tempo of habanera had quickened. It was now a new dance, the *milonga*—a purely African word, meaning "argument" or "issue" in Kimbundu and "lines of dancers" in Ki-Kongo.

pepper on it!") when the dancing is becoming desultory.

The history of tango music, too, traces a tumultuous sequence, from the earliest recordings to masters of the 1940s such as di Sarli, D'Arienzo, Troilo, Salgán, Pugliese, and Piazzolla. Salgán and Pugliese are world-class composers, and their works deserve the same degree of acclaim that their more renowned colleague Piazzolla has received. Salgán's "La llamo silbando" (I call her by whistling) and Pugliese's "Malandraca" (Woman delinquent) will doubtless become as famous as Piazzolla's "Adiós Nonino" (Farewell, Nonino) and "Tanguodia III." El Nuevo Quinteto Real, led by Salgán, and the Orquesta El Arranque, in differing ways, lead tango to the future. Meanwhile Gabriel Angio and Natalia Games have had the audacity to blend hip-hop downrock with traditional tango. When they pull off that blend, lucky the Bethlehem toward which they slouch.

Tango, as dance, in the phrasing of Cormac McCarthy, "contains within itself its own arrangement and history and finale." And the experts we honor, from whom we take counsel, are Argentine. To understand tango, we must go to Buenos Aires and follow women and men to their milongas, their schools of being, where the prose of human action becomes a poetry of valor, pleasure, and precision. ◉

Mariano Acosta,
2000.

HENRI CARTIER-BRESSON

THE GRACE OF INTUITION

n a strange rapture, a blind boy feels his way along a speckled wall. Two women at a transit camp for refugees in April 1945: one is a former Gestapo informer; the other, with an almost inhuman grimace, points her finger. Matisse, his back to the camera, draws a woman who is all sumptuous curls. A perfect moment behind the Gare Saint Lazare: a small flood, a clock in the distance, "RAILOWSKY," semicircles of debris, a man who jumps, his reflected jump. There is scarcely a new way to put it. Henri Cartier-Bresson's images *act*: they enter, lock into place, become part of what we are. Our eyes are moved through them as our ears are moved through Bach's counterpoint; it is a kind of synaesthesia. Cartier-Bresson refers to it as the instant of the "Golden Mean."

There are many reasons why Cartier-Bresson is one of the most influential photographers of our era. He was a founding member in 1947 of the Magnum Photos agency, which in many ways redefined the role of the photojournalist. His 1952 book *Images à la Sauvette*, or *The Decisive Moment*, proposed a new approach to "image-snatching" and made a deep and indelible impact on the medium. He has created unique visual documents of our world during a century of nearly imponderable change and upheaval.

But the chief reasons for Cartier-Bresson's effect on photography are, of course, the images themselves—produced (he asserts) simply by the grace of intuition, by *being there*, and sensing just when "everything falls into place." Taking a photograph, he once said, is "putting one's head, one's eye, and one's heart on the same axis." The axis sought and so often located by two of Cartier-Bresson's heroes, painters Paolo Uccello and Paul Cézanne. The result is something *elegant*, in the word's truest, most physical, and most profound sense.

In 1931, at the age of twenty-two, Cartier-Bresson left home and an unavoidable career in his family's textile business, and spent a year hunting in the West African bush. Photographs from this sojourn—some of his very earliest images—are shown in the following pages. While in the Ivory Coast, he contracted blackwater fever, and returned to France to convalesce. Cartier-Bresson had been an art student before leaving home; his instinctively acute eye was further sharpened under the tutelage of the painter André Lhote (whose image also appears here). But when he returned from Africa to Europe, Cartier-Bresson discovered a *new* way of observing—through his recently acquired Leica. He once described having "prowled the streets all day" in this period, "feeling very strung-up and ready to pounce, determined to 'trap' life, to preserve life in the act of living." For him, the camera became an *extension of the eye*.

The following decades provided Cartier-Bresson with ample ways and places to make use of this new mode of seeing. He traveled widely. He worked on films with Jean Renoir and, during a year in the United States, with Paul Strand. He volunteered in the Spanish Civil War. He escaped from a German POW camp in 1943 (after two unsuccessful attempts), and then joined the French Resistance. For a time after the war, his whereabouts were so uncertain that in 1946 New York's Museum of Modern Art organized a "posthumous" retrospective of his work. In 1954, he was the first foreign photographer to be admitted to the USSR. Indeed, he covered the globe: China, Burma, Pakistan, Indonesia, Japan, Canada, the United States, all of Europe   falling deeply in love with Mexico and India—and photographing at every step.

Then, in the early 1970s, having reached what might have been a pinnacle, Cartier-Bresson set his camera down, to devote the core of his creative energies to drawing—like photography, an intuitive medium, but according to Cartier-Bresson, a more "meditative" one.

Last year, Cartier-Bresson decided it was now time to show some of his photographic lifework that had not yet been made public. He has been generous enough to allow *Aperture* to publish some of this unseen work in these pages.

Now ninety-five years old, Cartier-Bresson is as engaged and active as he has ever been. At the time of this writing, he was

INTERVIEW BY DIANA C. STOLL

working hard to set up the new HCB Foundation, and planning a massive retrospective, curated by Robert Delpire and titled "De qui s'agit-il?" (cryptically: "Who is it about?"), at the Bibliothèque Nationale in Paris. Both are scheduled to open in April 2003.

The HCB Foundation—which has been in the works for many years—was initiated by Cartier-Bresson, his wife photographer Martine Franck, and their daughter Mélanie. Its purpose is to preserve and maintain Cartier-Bresson's work, which will be exhibited at the foundation's Paris headquarters along with the work of other artists. The foundation is also offering a biannual grant, the Grand Prix International Henri Cartier-Bresson, of 30,000 Euros to a deserving photographer or project nominated by a photography institution.

It might seem that this is a time of summation for Cartier-Bresson: putting things in order through his foundation, and organizing the retrospective show. But in this interview, he denies that there is anything "definitive" about his activities at this or any other point. (His responses to questions—like his eye—are quick and confident and unexpected.) "Life changes," he says succinctly; "death does not change." Rather than ruminating and summarizing, he prefers to be alive and reactive.

He once said: "Nothing is lost. All that you have ever seen is always with you." Nonetheless—or therefore—Cartier-Bresson is a man who tends not to look backwards.

DIANA C. STOLL: You've chosen now to show images that have not been previously published. What is it like for you to look back over your contact prints or negatives, and to make a new selection?

HENRI CARTIER-BRESSON: Contact sheets are like notes for a writer. For me, what is important is what is going to happen in the next moment: it is life that is in front of us. The word "definitive" has something morbid to it. I don't like to be passive, but rather to be alive and reacting. The beauty of form and geometry are what matters. You have to know, intuitively, where the golden rule falls.

DCS: Has your eye changed over the years?

HCB: To your question I would answer: only the gaze of a statue doesn't change. Life changes, death does not change. Seeing is questioning. There are few people that really *see*. Alberto Giacometti has clearly expressed himself on the subject. The majority of people think, but questioning vision is rarer. To see is sensitivity in relation to shape and geometry.

DCS: You have photographed all over the world. How much do you think place affects your photographs? Is it all equally familiar—or equally foreign—to you?

HCB: Nothing is really familiar. One is always looking for surprises in whatever country one is in. But I have always tried to avoid being part of the *nomenklatura*, to avoid entering into the "system." I've tried to remain perpetually "on the run and on the go."

DCS: That is maybe why your eye has remained so agile.

HCB: The important question is: "What is it all about?" And there is no definitive answer, only new questions.

DCS: What took you to the Ivory Coast in 1931? Do you recall your impressions of the place?

HCB: I went to the Ivory Coast to avoid entering the family textile business. I had the chance to go on a cargo boat to Cameroon, but I disembarked from the boat in the Ivory Coast as I did not want to return to Europe. I earned my living hunting—I crossed the Coraly River to buy ammunition in Liberia. It was the Africa I had read about in Joseph Conrad's *Heart of Darkness*.

I was embarrassed to be white there, on account of the exploitation of the Africans by the colonialists. I caught blackwater fever and wanted to die in Africa . . . fortunately, I was cured—not by an Occidental doctor, but by local magic, the village witch doctors.

DCS: Your images from postwar New York in 1947 depict a distinctly "American" place—the photographs here are filled with movement, easy gestures. How did America strike you, as a Frenchman and a photographer, at that point in time?

(continued on page 52)

PAGE 44: Self-Portrait, France, 1932; ABOVE: Barrio Chino, Barcelona, 1932.

Mexico, 1934.

Saratoga, New York, 1947.

France, ca. 1936.

Stratford-upon-Avon,
Warwickshire,
England, 1953.

(continued from page 46) **HCB**: I lived in Harlem and then on 23rd Street. The vitality of New York impressed me. It was thanks to the Americans that I became known as a photographer: Monroe Wheeler, Lincoln Kirstein, Nancy and Beaumont Newhall and the Museum of Modern Art gave me my first exhibition in 1947.

DCS: This was the show that was originally planned as a "posthumous" exhibition?

HCB: There was a confusion: Wheeler, Kirstein, and the Newhalls thought that I had died during the Second World War. They were very polite and courteous, though: when they found out that I was alive they didn't *require* that the show be posthumous!

DCS: You've referred to India and Mexico as two "havens for your heart." What respite did you find in those countries? How did that sense translate into your photographs?

HCB: India and Mexico are the two countries where I feel completely at ease—despite my Anglo-Saxon looks. I always liked their conception of life, which was in complete opposition to Parisian life. My love of those two countries does not go through the brain but through my bloodstream—an "osmosis." These two civilizations formed me.

DCS: How does this "osmosis" take place—how are things created without traveling through the brain?

HCB: It is sight that directs me. It is the instantaneous side of photography that fascinates me, while drawing is a meditation. Photography is when the subject comes out at you, while drawing is intuitive and meditative. There are to my knowledge no "sensibility professors."

   Color is another problem. Address Poussin, Cézanne, Matisse, Giacometti on the subject of color.

DCS: You've spoken and been asked many times about photography versus drawing. "Photography," you've said, "is an immediate reaction, drawing is a meditation." Could you talk about why you've devoted your energy in recent years so much to the latter?

HCB: Actually, I still take portraits of my friends—what Giacometti called "*faire des têtes*" ("doing heads"). In drawing, it is your finger that is in command; with photography it is your nostrils that tell you where to go (intuition).

DCS: The Golden Mean, Uccello, Cézanne: What is *elegance* in an image? What distinguishes those who achieve it?

HCB: *Elegance* is a word frequently used by mathematicians. In a photograph, I suppose one could say it is when, intuitively, everything falls into place.

DCS: There is a major retrospective of your work coming up in Paris—could you tell us about it?

HCB: The retrospective will open at the Bibliothèque Nationale in Paris in April and will run until the end of July. It's called "De qui s'agit-il?" and will show previously unexhibited and unpublished material: vintage and unpublished prints, publications, family photographs, drawings, films. . . . It's being put together by the HCB Foundation and Robert Delpire.

DCS: You've had many collaborations with Delpire over the years—you must have established a wonderful working rapport. I imagine the upcoming retrospective is presenting some difficult decisions.

HCB: Tériade and Delpire were both very important for me. I owe a lot to Bob Delpire. I have a great intimacy and friendship with him; he has a very sharp eye, intuition, sensitivity, and a feeling for composition. He is gifted as a great editor.

DCS: Do you continue to find surprise? What else do you look for and hope for?

HCB: Of course. Life is continually a surprise. I am still looking for a certain geometry. The Golden Mean. ◌

"Henri Cartier-Bresson: De qui s'agit-il?" is being presented at the Bibliothèque Nationale's Site François-Mitterrand in Paris, April 29–July 31, 2003. Cartier-Bresson was awarded the first Aperture/Michael E. Hoffman Award for photographic achievement in January 2003.

Hyderabad, Pakistan,
1947–48.

Ivory Coast, 1931.

Poland, 1931.

France, 1938.

Ivory Coast, 1931.

Paris, 1932.

The Embankment, London, 1951.

BY FRED RITCHIN

THE UNBEARABLE RELEVANCE OF PHOTOGRAPHY

1968

jacques borel
WILLPY
ANCRE PILS
RHUME
ATTENDEZ
PIETONS

Thirty-five years ago, protest was in the air and on the streets. But unlike today, the photographer was essential to the depiction and interpretation of the turmoil that swirled about.

Looking at the photographs from 1968 is an exercise in nostalgia. Not only because people are depicted fighting to claim control of their own destinies against repressive governments, but also because the photographs themselves were key to mobilizing popular sentiment. It was a time when the photograph was considered a pivotal social catalyst and not, as often is the case today, the pawn of a system intent on fabricating pseudo-realities.

It was a different universe, a Newtonian one where actions such as the killing of Dr. Martin Luther King, Jr., or the summary execution of a Vietcong prisoner led to intense and diverse reactions. There were massive riots and peace marches. Many people refused to fight in a war, and others volunteered to fight all the harder. Photographs, along with the emerging medium of television, helped to change opinions and reorient perspectives.

The photograph served as social intermediary. It interpreted events as a way of publicizing and confirming them, and then recorded popular reactions, emboldening the participants in part by ensuring their entry into collective history. In contrast to today, the photograph was received much more as a translucent window than as a distorting mirror, giving it a place of power and privilege in people's evolving belief systems.

Photography became, even before the advent of the computer popularized the term, an *interactive* family album. It showed a world in distress, but it did not stop there: implicit in the publication of an image was the sense that its diffusion might lead to

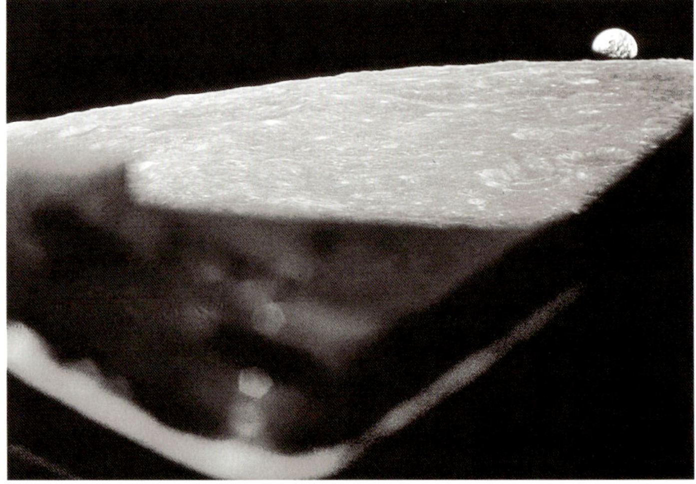

the amelioration of the situation depicted. A searing image of the famine in Biafra could lead to an international outcry for hunger relief; a photograph of the earth as seen from outer space could and did spark a global movement to save the planet. Social and political reform seemed possible globally and not just locally, as in the earlier days of Lewis Hine or Dorothea Lange.

Before the age of widespread jet travel or the omnipresence of CNN, the photograph provided a singular purview onto far-flung realities. There were events and places depicted that one had no hope of ever personally experiencing, making the photographic interpretation seem largely incontrovertible. As such, photography had a power to shock, to upset its audience because it created an alternative discourse that was difficult to downplay. The foreignness of the imagery, its exotic nature, added to photography's visceral impact rather than eroding it.

In 1968 photography was also particularly effective at interrogating the official narratives provided by governments. The American athletes giving a Black Power salute at the Olympics, or the dead civilians in My Lai (the images would be published later), or the students in the streets of Paris and Mexico demonstrated that the official versions of events could be effectively contradicted. Photography was arguing for *complexity* as a consequence of the need to understand.

Today's bleak, unrelentingly grim photographic record of calamity is rooted not in a Newtonian universe but in a more unbending world of chaos. The images have become disconnected from the events they depict, informed more by the manipulative strategies of those in power, whether governments or media corporations, than by any moral compass. Contemporary photographs constitute more of a **(continued on page 70)**

PREVIOUS PAGES:
Bruno Barbey, Students
hurling projectiles against the
riot police. Boulevard Saint
Germain, Paris, May 6, 1968.

OPPOSITE, LEFT
Eddie Adams, South
Vietnamese National Police
Chief Brigadier General Nguyen
Ngoc Loan executes a Vietcong
officer with a single pistol
shot in the head. Saigon,
February 1, 1968.

OPPOSITE, RIGHT·
View of the rising Earth, viewed
from Apollo 8. December 1968.

LEFT:
Roger Malloch, Anti–Vietnam
War protest during the
Democratic National
Convention. At center:
American writers William
Burroughs and Allen Ginsberg.
Chicago, August 1968.

ABOVE:
Extending gloved fists
skyward in racial protest, U.S.
athletes Tommie Smith (center)
and John Carlos (right) look
down as "The Star Spangled
Banner" is played. Smith had
just received the gold medal
and Carlos the bronze for the
two-hundred-meter run at the
Summer Olympic Games in
Mexico City. Australian silver
medalist Peter Norman is at
left. October 16, 1968.
(Photographer unknown.)

RIGHT:
Li Zhensheng, In a public trial, eight are sentenced to death and executed for counter-revolutionary activities. Harbin, Heilongjiang Province, China, April 5, 1968.

BELOW:
Don McCullin, Waiting for food distribution in a Catholic mission. Biafra, 1968.

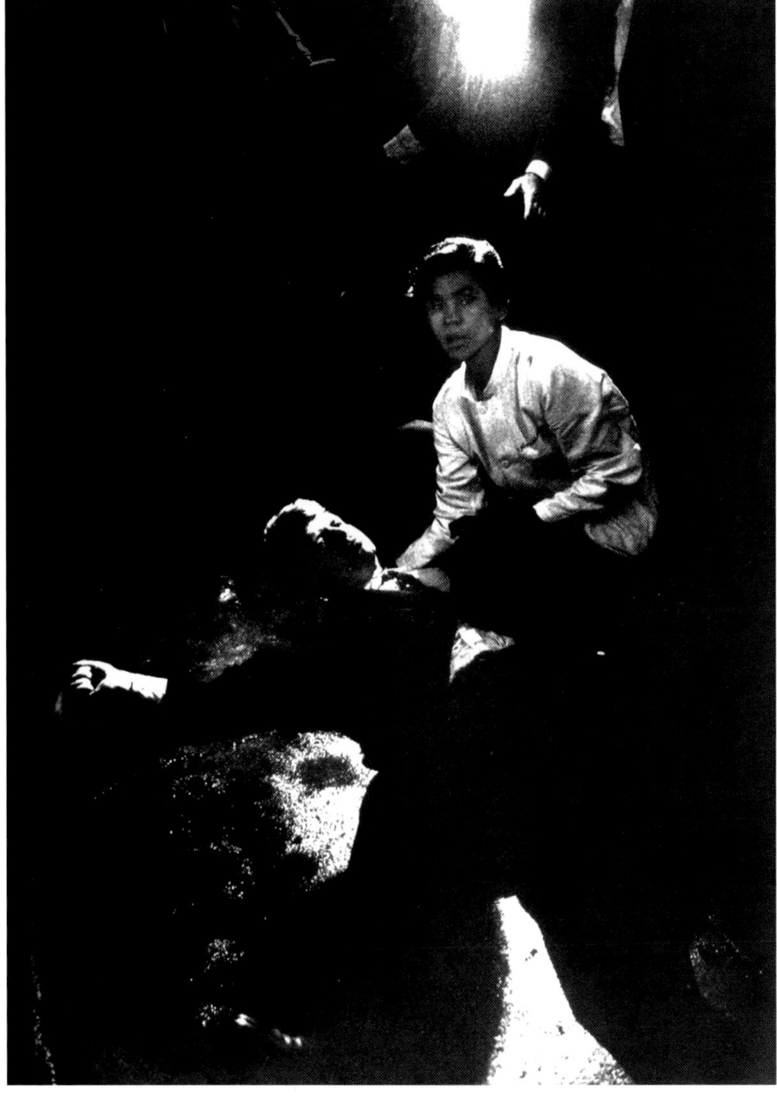

ABOVE:
Li Zhensheng, Swimmers along Songhuajiang River commemorate the second anniversary of Mao's swim in the Yangtze; here, they are studying Mao's works before going into the water. Harbin, Heilongjiang Province, China, July 16, 1968.

LEFT:
Bill Eppridge, Senator Robert Kennedy sprawled semiconscious after being shot, as busboy Juan Romero tries to comfort him. Los Angeles, June 5, 1968.

Gilles Carone, During student
riots in Mexico City.
September 1968.

ABOVE:
Hiroji Hamaya, During
protests of Tokyo
University students.
January 18, 1968.

RIGHT, TOP:
Don McCullin,
The Beatles, 1968.

RIGHT, BOTTOM:
Jack Thornell,
A police officer swings
a nightstick at an alleged
looter during racial violence
that erupted at a civil
rights march in Memphis.
March 28, 1968.

LEFT:
Elliott Erwitt, At the Republican National Convention.
Miami, August, 1968.

ABOVE: Black Panther leader Eldridge Cleaver, presidential candidate on the Peace and Freedom Party ticket, stands beside his bullet riddled campaign poster in the window of the Black Panther headquarters. Oakland, September 11, 1968. (Photographer unknown.)

BELOW:
Constantine Manos, Coretta Scott King and her children stand by the open coffin of her husband, Martin Luther King, Jr. Atlanta, April 9, 1968.

(continued from page 64) stenography of the morgue than a family album. Each image, if not of a suicide bombing or some other carnage, is limned by the global tilt toward self-induced destruction. Few photographs, other than the most naïve, are linked even potentially to social amelioration or more broadly to hope. This explains why so many photographers now vie to work with human-rights organizations while abandoning the mass media that they feel is abandoning them.

Our vocabulary of imagery in mass media has consequently shrunk as we have abandoned the interrogatory form for the knee-jerk affirmation and for quick resolutions to our dilemmas. The destruction of the Twin Towers made for riveting imagery, but resulted in a series of instant histories whose intent was to produce immediate icons of the event. These icons, revolving around an amalgam of the Christian cross and American flag-raising, were provided to replace doubt with the reward of instantaneous resurrection. We barely had time to grieve.

It was a tactic that has encouraged a simplistic worldview of Good against Evil. Rather than a proliferation of images exploring cultural differences and possible injustices that might have incited such a heinous attack, we were shown a war against terrorism that reached, unsuccessfully, for the unequivocal iconography of World War II. The visualization of the war has been sidetracked into the metaphor of a video game. It was not a new strategy, but the continuation of the "cyber-photography" that reached consciousness during the Persian Gulf War, when "smart bombs" and battlefield simulations replaced the largely interrogatory photography that surfaced passionately in 1968 (and began with Robert Frank a decade earlier). This imagery of interrogation, questioning the distribution of power and its legitimacy, took us through the conflict in Vietnam and through the end of the Cold War.

The landmark 1967 exhibition at New York's Museum of Modern Art, "New Documents," curated by John Szarkowski and featuring the work of Diane

TOP: Constantine Manos, Poor People's March. Washington D.C., June, 1968;
ABOVE: Don McCullin, Father and child, wounded when U.S. Marines dropped hand grenades into their shelter, during the Tet Offensive. Hue, Vietnam, 1968.

LEFT:
Elliot Landy, Bob Dylan at home. Byrdcliff,
New York, 1968.

ABOVE:
Demonstrators from the National Women's Liberation
Party picket with signs in protest of the annual
Miss America Pageant. Atlantic City, N.J.,
September 7, 1968. (Photographer unknown.)

ABOVE: Raymond Depardon, National Guardsman at the Democratic National Convention. Chicago, August, 1968.

Arbus, Lee Friedlander, and Garry Winogrand, dramatically previewed an eventual shift by a generation of self-motivated, independent documentarians to a more sardonic stance regarding society. For the mass media, the fall of the Berlin Wall over two decades later was a marker of, among many other things, the erosion of such irony. It signaled the end of the era of multiple truths, when there were always at least two sides to any story, and the beginning of an overarching official point of view against which all other perspectives would be measured. Now there could be only one super power, and one image: the *official* one.

Since then photography has been looking for its voice, less able to contest official visions with any alternative version but the most personal. To a logical mind it is difficult to resolve the constant paradox that each side in a conflict might be both right and wrong, that everyone's grievances might have merit, that violence can be both random and horrific and yet still somehow justified. Photographers, like the rest of us, find it difficult to take sides when good and bad are so intrinsically relative. And we turn from the evidence of their images because, unlike in 1968, few have any sense as to what political or moral benefit confronting it might have.

This is why we comb the world for visions by photographers from other, less "empowered" places, who might have more profound, digestible insights, or images by children or the blind or the elderly or the insane, who might have something substantive to add. Photography is no longer a common language depicting distress through the filter of hope. It will never be a universal language, but right now it is increasingly a dormant one. The

managers of mass media, terrified of photography's capacity for disquieting ambiguities and irresolvable questions, prefer to illustrate bromides, expecting that the photographic act will somehow sustain the idiocy of the invention. One hopes that those intent on expanding photography's vocabulary, its reach, the individuals working on the margins, will provide some new and challenging perspectives.

Certainly the photographs from 1968 provided no panacea. But in the medium of the mass, at least for the moment, the photograph has started to closely resemble a caged bird. ◉

OPPOSITE, TOP: Josef Koudelka, Invasion of Warsaw Pact troops. Prague, August, 1968; OPPOSITE, BOTTOM: Don McCullin, Shell-shocked soldier awaits transportation away from front line during the Tet Offensive. Hue, Vietnam, 1968; ABOVE: Raymond Depardon, Republican presidential candidate Richard Nixon campaigning. Sioux City, Iowa, October 1968.

MANUEL ALVAREZ BRAVO, 1902–2002

Obsessed by mythology, Manuel Alvarez Bravo led a legendary life. Haunted by history, he became it. Entranced by all he saw, he created a way of seeing.

He was a street photographer, a portraitist, a surrealist, an experimentalist, a creator of iconic landscapes, still lifes, and nudes. He brought Mexican photography out from the long shadows of Agustín Casasola and Hugo Brehme. He paved the way for Flor Garduño and Graciela Iturbide.

He was one of the great Modernists. He knew everybody. Tina Modotti adored him, Edward Weston admired him. He drank cognac with José Clemente Orozco, ate Chinese food with Henri Cartier-Bresson. He shot motion pictures with Luis Buñuel, went to the openings with Rufino Tamayo, listened to Diego Rivera talk politics. He knew Leon Trotsky, collaborated with Octavio Paz.

He married strong, talented women. First was Lola Alvarez Bravo, then Doris Heyden, then Colette Urbajtel.

He grew up in Mexico City and he never left. As a kid on his way to school he often tripped over dead soldiers the Mexican Revolution had left rotting on his neighborhood streets. As an old man he could sit for hours in the center of his living room on rainy afternoons, transported by the voice of Caruso.

He wore a serape with his business suit, was equal parts proletarian and epicurean. He collected Callas and Pavarotti, Mahler and Debussy, Spanish ballads and Yiddish folk songs. He loved to read Joyce, Dostoevsky, and Proust; loved to quote Sor Juana Inés de la Cruz. And Cervantes was always with him. "The figure of Quixote," he once said, "is extraordinary."

He loved painting, had his own Pablo O'Higgins and Dr. Atl. He loved the photographs of Berenice Abbott, Albert Renger-Patzsch, Eugène Atget, August Sander, Josef Koudelka, Minor White, Nadar, Muybridge, and more.

Art, he asserted, had nothing to do with favorites. "If I am looking at an El Greco, Picasso doesn't matter to me. If I am looking at a painting of Clemente Orozco or at an engraving by Rembrandt—at that moment I prefer them to all others."

The same can be said of the master's own work. For the moment we gaze at *Angeles en camion* (Angels in a truck), *Obrero en huelga, asesinado* (Striking worker, assassinated), *Caja de Visiones* (Box of visions), *El umbral* (Threshold), or any number of his other optical parables, nothing else really matters. The images seduce us without show, enrapture us without allusion, each one a world complete unto itself.

He made his first photographs when he was a teenager, images of the beggars who lingered on the steps of the Catholic church around the block from his house. He surged to national

ABOVE: Mary Ellen Mark, *Manuel Alvarez Bravo*, Mexico, 1988; OPPOSITE: Manuel Alvarez Bravo, *La hija de los danzantes* (Daughter of the dancers), Cholula, Puebla, Mexico, 1933.

prominence in 1931, when he won first prize in a competition sponsored by the company, La Tolteca. He reached an American audience in 1953, featured on the cover of *Aperture*.

He exhibited from Paris to Moscow, Helsinki to Caracas, São Paolo to Shanghai. He won Mexico's National Art Prize, Sweden's Hasselblad Prize, a Leica Medal of Excellence, and was honored by the International Center of Photography as a Master of Photography. In the final years of his life, his eyesight virtually obliterated, he still carried a camera.

People who knew him will remember his soft voice, his infatuation with riddles and alchemy, his vast knowledge of anthropology and technical gadgetry. They will remember the mathematical precision of his conversation, his quick eye, his white gloves. Those who never met him will remember his images of Mexico in all its glory and futility, subtlety and extravagance, its profound carnival of fleshly ghosts and ghostly flesh.

Don Manuel distrusted superlatives as much as he detested pretension. So let us salute him by simply saying he loved art and he loved his country. From the beginning to the end of the twentieth century, he was a photographer. ⊙

—Frederick Kaufman

SELECTED BOOKS

EXCERPTS

CZECH PHOTOGRAPHIC AVANT-GARDE 1918–1948

Edited by Vladimír Birgus
Cambridge, MA: MIT Press, 2002

Poetism culminated during the latter half of the 1920s as an artistic movement, not merely as a vital principle. Its intricate development was almost concurrent with that of the Czech avant-garde. The main theoretical representatives of Devětsil, Vítězslav Nezal and Karel Teige, devoted a special issue of *ReD* to the move-

(continued on next page)

**Trudy Wilner Stack
WINOGRAND 1964**

Santa Fe: Arena Editions, 2002

Winogrand photographed what amazed him and aroused his interest. Each picture was a formal translation of "Look at that!" Once they were photographs in his hands, the good ones held even more welcome surprises, but not accidents. His best pictures, and there are mountains of them, are the result of a radically disciplined photographic intelligence charged with animal alertness. Life falls together within these frames, defying the very complexity and chance they can suggest. While stereotypes may have been triggers—cowboys, Blacks, tourists, blond children, certain kinds of women

(continued on next page)

**Jonathan Williams
A PALPABLE ELYSIUM:
PORTRAITS OF GENIUS
AND SOLITUDE**

Boston: David R. Godine, 2002

***On Aaron Siskind:*
All my favorite avuncular adjectives trot forth when I think about Aaron Siskind: *kindly, astute, enthusiastic, loyal, uproarious, masterly.* Has there ever been a greater photographer? To ask that excessive question is not to**

(continued on next page)

A Palpable Elysium **continued**

diminish the tremendous range of Paul Strand or the depth of feeling in Stieglitz or Sudek. I merely suggest that Siskind could mount 400 prints on the wall and not show us one second-rate image. . . . I remember a famous Siskind statement: "When you photograph a wall, you photograph a wall. When I photograph a wall, I'm photographing something else." Namely: Aaron Siskind. He wrote to me very recently: "I still love travelling. When I visit a new country, I find old Siskind there."

On Ralph Eugene Meatyard: He could make *anything* strange, even Lexington.

I continue to muse upon, be amazed by, be amused by, this singular photographer as much as anyone I have ever known. Not that anyone ever got to know much. Haunted houses don't release press releases.

He was terribly kind, terribly talented. In a way, as remarkable a man with a camera as we have ever had. Henry Holmes Smith told me to go see him in 1960. I did. I am so glad I had the simple gumption to do so. Usually, we never do what our betters suggest.

Czech Avant Garde **continued**
ment, published under the general title "Poetist Manifestos" (*ReD* no.9, 1928). In doing this, they extended the validity of the Poetist platform until around 1930, at which point it became clear that this barely two-year-old declaration would have to be revised in view of the development in European art and politics. Poetism began somewhat to impede the reception of Surrealism, whose manifestos had been the subject of debate in Bohemia since 1924; Surrealism was not accepted as

an artistic program by former Devětsil members until 1934, however. During the period 1929–1933, Nezval, Teige, and Štyrsky initially looked askance at Surrealism: they rejected its historicism, narrative character, mythology and Romanticism as well as the return to illusionistic depictions of the three-dimensional world. To the representatives of Poetism, Surrealism was by no means a modern movement, as it had not arisen from the devastation of the war to critically re-examine the status of art before 1914; further, it did not renounce psychologism, and made open reference to sources from the 19th century.

—*Karel Srp*

Winogrand **continued**
(housewives, beauty queens, drive-in dates)—his figures present themselves with equal authority and wholeness. "He tests our stereotypes of race (a very dangerous game), he doesn't valorize Blacks, he presents them as woven into his pictures, part of the continuum," says photographer and Winogrand friend Tod Papageorge. But especially in Texas, the question of race in America looms, as does the role and image of women, the nature of relationships between parents and children, and the culpable/vulnerable/venerable white male authority. He was not immune to it, but he would not be responsible for it.

If his subjects often maintain a certain unalterable presence and control over their identity as they brave the public sphere, Winogrand also takes full advantage of events where life begins to play itself in a popular theater of parades and sports, fairs and stage shows—all-American entertainments, sales pitches, and celebrations.

INGE MORATH, 1923—2002

Inge Morath, who died on January 30, 2002, brought all her vibrancy and keen intelligence to the photographs she took over the course of half a century. The luminous, joyful quality of her pictures directly reflects the synthesis of her public and personal life. A woman of exceptional graciousness and talent, she is greatly missed not only by the Aperture Foundation, which published Morath's *Portraits* in 1986 and *Russian Journal* in 1991, but by everyone she befriended during her long and fruitful career. She enriched us all.

Morath was born in Austria in 1923, and as a child she moved to Germany with her parents, Protestant liberals and research scientists. At the outbreak of World War II she was studying languages at Berlin University. When Morath refused to become a Nazi supporter, she was assigned to forced labor, assembling airplane parts at Templehof airport, a site that was being repeatedly bombed by the Allies. She escaped from Templehof when an air raid blew open the gate, and found her way through war-torn Europe back to her family in Austria. The trauma of war remained with her for life, the horror of what she had seen returning whenever she talked about it.

Upon Morath's graduation from university in 1944, she was fluent in German, French, English, and Spanish, and through the years acquired other languages, including Mandarin, Russian, and Romanian. After the war she worked as an interpreter for the United States Information Service, and then wrote for the Austrian radio network Rot-Weiss-Rot. She also contributed to *Der Optimist*, a literary magazine. She wrote captions and stories for photographer Ernst Haas, a fellow Austrian based in Paris. There, Morath encountered a group of young photographers who had founded the photography agency Magnum. She became the agency's researcher, writer, and editor—the career she had envisioned during her university years.

In 1951 Morath moved to London, where she picked up a camera and began adding visual imagery to her love of language and literature, studying under Simon Guttman, the legendary editor of *Picture Post*. Two years later she became an assistant to Henri Cartier-Bresson, and soon after made her own photographic mark with pictures from a journey to Spain. *Guerre à la Tristesse/Fiesta in Pamplona*, 1955, launched a series of books on her far-flung travels in Europe, the Middle East, North Africa, and eventually China and Russia. Robert Capa invited her to join Magnum as a full member in 1955.

In 1960 Cartier-Bresson and Morath went to the Nevada desert to shoot stills and photograph on the set of John Huston's film *The Misfits*, which Arthur Miller had written for his then wife Marilyn Monroe. Although Morath had seen a production of *The Crucible* in Paris, this was her first meeting with Miller himself. They married in 1962, settling in New York and Roxbury, Connecticut. Their life became a rich collaboration of spirit and art, family and travel. Together they produced such books as *In Russia*, 1969, and *Chinese Encounters*, 1979, with Miller's text and Morath's photographs. Many of their Connecticut neighbors sat for her camera—Alexander Calder, Philip Roth, William Styron, and Honor Moore among them. Their daughter Rebecca, now a writer and

film director, is married to actor Daniel Day-Lewis.

Morath photographed with consummate astuteness to the situation and respect for the individual. Her pictures are unobtrusively composed, allowing a sense of spontaneity, and sometimes playful humor. Her famous series of the paper masks that Saul Steinberg created, worn by his wife and friends— and eventually anyone Morath thought might provide a good torso for a fanciful head—is an exploration of physical abstraction and dislocation in ordinary life, as well as a great deal of fun. They form the center of her book *Portraits*, flanked by images of some of the many writers, performers, and artists she photographed: Anaïs Nin, Jason Robards, Bernard Buffet, Dustin Hoffman, Octavio Paz, André Malraux, Victoria Sackville-West, Eleanor Roosevelt, Adlai Stevenson, and many other luminaries. The same volume includes a portrait, made with equal consideration and tenderness, of a farmer relaxing in his flower-papered parlor, eyes attentive to the camera, the cord of his hearing aid snaking from shirt pocket to ear.

"I will always remain curious about people," Morath wrote in her notes at the end of *Portraits*. "I like to photograph them in the places where they live or where they spend much of their time, places that have absorbed something of their person. . . . No encounter is the same as another. The final, wonderful surprise is always the person itself."

And so it was with Inge Morath: no encounter was ever the same; her pictures and her life were always a wonderful surprise. ⌾

—Rebecca Busselle

CONTRIBUTORS' BIOS

VINCE ALETTI is the art editor and photography critic for the *Village Voice*, and a regular contributor to *Artforum* magazine. He was the co-editor of *Aperture*'s issue "Male/Female," which featured his interview with Madonna, and an essayist for *The Book of 101 Books: Seminal Photographic Books of the Twentieth Century* (Ruth Horowitz, LLC/PPP Editions, in collaboration with DAP, 2001).

REBECCA BUSSELLE is the author of three books: *An Exposure of the Heart*, *Bathing Ugly*, and *Frog's-Eye View*. She is a former *Aperture* editor.

ROSELEE GOLDBERG, cultural critic, curator, and producer, pioneered the study of performance art with her seminal book *Performance Art from Futurism to the Present*, first published in 1979. She is a frequent contributor to *Artforum*, and her publications include *Performance Since 1960* (1998) and *Laurie Anderson* (2000). Goldberg teaches at New York University.

FREDERICK KAUFMAN's most recent book, *Manuel Alvarez Bravo: Photographs and Memories*, was published by *Aperture* in 1997.

FRED RITCHIN is acting chair of the Photography & Imaging Department at New York University's Tisch School of the Arts, director of PixelPress (www.pixelpress.org), and author of the forthcoming *Reinventing Photography*. He remembers 1968 fondly.

DIANA C. STOLL is Editor at Large of *Aperture* magazine.

FRONT COVER: Henri Cartier-Bresson, New York City, 1947.

ROBERT FARRIS THOMPSON is the Colonel John Trumbull Professor of the History of Art at Yale. He is the author of ten books, including the recent *Le Geste Kongo*, published in Paris, September 2002. Thompson's text in this issue is excerpted from his forthcoming book *Tango: Black Gift*.

LARRY TOWELL has been a full member of the Magnum Photos agency since 1993. Among his many books are *Then Palestine* (Aperture, 1999) and *The Mennonites* (Phaidon, 2000). A new volume, *The World From My Front Porch*, is forthcoming.

LARRY TOWELL

ADRIANA GROISMAN

ANDREA MODICA

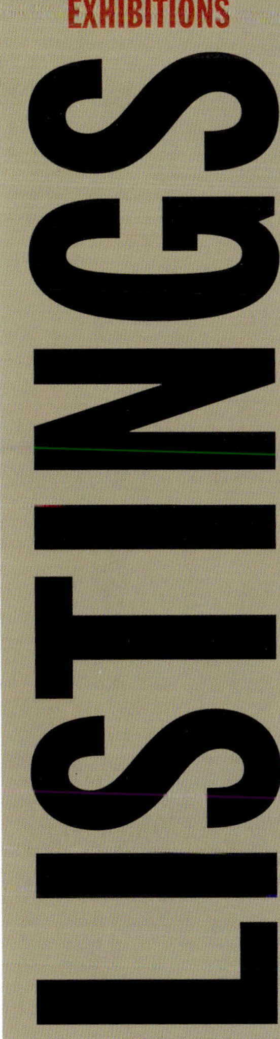

UPCOMING SELECTED EXHIBITIONS

USA

ALBUQUERQUE, NM
*New Mexico Museum of Natural History, *Michael Nichols:Brutal Kinship* March 22–June 14, 2003

ATLANTA, GA
The High Museum of Art *Land of Myth and Memory: Clarence John Laughlin and Photographers of the South* January 25–August 9, 2003

CASPER, WY
*Nicolaysen Art Museum *Charles Lindsay: Upstream: Fly Fishing in the American West* May 16–September 7, 2003

CHICAGO, IL
The Art Institute of Chicago *Unknown Maker: The Art of the American Daguerreotype* June 21–September 28, 2003

Museum of Contemporary Art *Thomas Struth: Picturing the World* June 28–September 28, 2003

Museum of Contemporary Photography *The Furtive Gaze* May 8–July 12, 2003

KNOXVILLE, TN
*Knoxville Museum of Art *Michiko Kon: Still Lifes* March 21–July 6, 2003

MILWAUKEE, WI
*Milwaukee Art Museum *Graciela Iturbide: Images of the Spirit* March 21–June 1, 2003

NEW YORK, NY
Grey Art Gallery, New York University *Swiss Peaks: Contemporary Swiss Photography* April 15–July 19, 2003

Metropolitan Museum of Art *The Photography of Charles Sheeler* June 3–August 17, 2003

Museum of Modern Art *Ansel Adams at 100* July–November 2003

OAKLAND, CA
Oakland Museum of California *Reflections in Black: Art and Activism* June 7–August 31, 2003

PHILADELPHIA, PA
Philadelphia Museum of Art *Louis Faurer Retrospective* June 14–September 7, 2003

PORTLAND, OR
Portland Museum of Art *Edward Weston: Life and Work* June 28–October 19, 2003

SAN DIEGO, CA
Museum of Photographic Arts *First Photographs: William Henry Fox Talbot and the Birth of Photography* March 30–June 15, 2003

In Talbot's Time: The First Twenty-Five Years of Photography March 30–June 8, 2003

SAN FRANCISCO, CA
San Francisco Museum of Modern Art *Picturing Modernity* Ongoing exhibition

Yerba Buena Center for the Arts *Time After Time: Asia and Our Moment* April 26–July 13, 2003

TUCSON, AZ
Margrethe Mather & Edward Weston: A Passionate Collaboration July 19–October 12, 2003

OUTSIDE USA

TORONTO, CANADA
Stephen Bulger Gallery *Magnum Photographers* May 10–June 14, 2003

LONDON, ENGLAND
National Portrait Gallery *Julia Margaret Cameron* February 6–May 26, 2003

Tate Modern *Photographs of the Twentieth Century* June 5–September 7, 2003

*An Aperture traveling exhibition.

CREDITS Unless otherwise noted, all photographs and texts are courtesy and copyright © the artists/or authors, all rights reserved. Pages 8, 10, and 12, all photographs courtesy Solomon R. Guggenheim Museum, New York; pp. 14–27, all photographs courtesy and copyright © Larry Towell/Magnum Photos, Inc.; pp. 15–19, excerpts from "Jenin: IDF Military Operations," courtesy and copyright © 2002 Human Rights Watch; pp. 34–43, all photographs courtesy and copyright © Adriana Groisman/Contact Press Images; pp. 44–61, all photographs courtesy and copyright © Henri Cartier-Bresson/Magnum Photos, Inc.; pp. 62–63, photograph by Bruno Barbey (cropped), courtesy and copyright © Bruno Barbey/Magnum Photos, Inc.; p. 64 (top), photograph courtesy and copyright © AP/Wide World Photos; p. 64 (bottom), photograph by Eddie Adams, courtesy and copyright © AP/Wide World Photos; p. 65, photograph by Roger Malloch, courtesy and copyright © Roger Malloch/Magnum Photos, Inc.; p. 65 (right), photograph courtesy and copyright © AP/Wide World Photos; p. 66 (left), photograph by Don McCullin, courtesy and copyright © Don McCullin/Contact Press Images; p. 66 (top and right), photographs by Li Zhensheng, courtesy and copyright © Li Zhensheng/Contact Press Images; p. 66 (bottom), photograph by Bill Eppridge, courtesy and copyright © Bill Eppridge/Timepix; p. 67, photograph by Gilles Carone, courtesy and copyright © Gilles Carone/Contact Press Images; p. 68 (left), photograph by Hiroji Hamaya, courtesy and copyright © Hiroji Hamaya/ Magnum Photos Inc.; p. 68 (top), photograph by Don McCullin, courtesy and copyright © Don McCullin/Contact Press Images; p. 68 (bottom), photograph courtesy and copyright © AP/Wide World Photos; p. 69 (top left), photograph by Elliott Erwitt, courtesy and copyright © Elliott Erwitt/Magnum Photos, Inc.; p. 69 (top right), photograph courtesy and copyright © AP/Wide World Photos; p. 69 (bottom), photograph by Constantine Manos (cropped), courtesy and copyright © Constantine Manos/Magnum Photos, Inc.; p. 70 (top), photograph by Constantine Manos, courtesy and copyright © Constantine Manos/Magnum Photos, Inc.; p. 70 (bottom), photograph by Don McCullin, courtesy and copyright © Don McCullin/Contact Press Images; p. 71 (left), photograph by Elliot Landy, courtesy and copyright © Elliot Landy/Magnum Photos, Inc.; p. 71 (right), photograph courtesy and copyright © AP/Wide World Photos; p. 71 (bottom), photograph by Raymond Depardon, courtesy and copyright © Raymond Depardon/Magnum Photos, Inc.; p. 72 (top), photograph by Josef Koudelka, courtesy and copyright © Josef Koudelka/Magnum Photos, Inc.; p. 72 (bottom), photograph by Don McCullin, courtesy and copyright © Don McCullin/Contact Press Images, Inc.; pp. 72–73, photograph by Raymond Depardon (cropped), courtesy and copyright © Raymond Depardon/Magnum Photos, Inc.; p. 75 (book covers), *A Palpable Elysium*, Boston: David R Godine, 2002; *Czech Photographic Avant-Garde 1918–1948*, Cambridge, MA: MIT Press, 2002; *Winogrand 1964*, Santa Fe: Arena Editions, 2002; pp. 76–77, photographs by Inge Morath, courtesy and copyright © Inge Morath Estate/Magnum Photos, Inc.; p. 80 (left), photograph by Paul Strand, copyright © Aperture Foundation, Inc./Paul Strand Archive.

ARTISTS IN THIS ISSUE INCLUDE: Marina Abramovic, Eddie Adams, Bruno Barbey, Bernd and Hilla Becher, Manuel Alvarez Bravo, Henri Cartier-Bresson, Gilles Carone, Gregory Crewdson, Raymond Depardon, Rineke Dijkstra, Bill Eppridge, Elliott Erwitt, Adriana Groisman, Hiroji Hamaya, Candida Höfer, Josef Koudelka, Elliot Landy, Roger Malloch, Constantine Manos, Mary Ellen Mark, Don McCullin, Andrea Modica, Inge Morath, Paul Strand, Larry Towell, Sam Taylor Wood, Marcos Vilariño, Li Zhensheng

TO SUBSCRIBE: *Aperture* (ISSN 0003-6420) is published quarterly, in spring, summer, fall, and winter, at 20 East 23rd Street, New York, NY 10010. A one-year subscription (four issues) is $40 and a two-year subscription (eight issues) is $66. A subscription for four issues outside the United States is $60. Single copies may be purchased at $18.50 for most issues. Periodicals postage is paid at New York and additional offices. Postmaster: Send address changes to *Aperture*, P.O. Box 3000, Denville, NJ 07834. Address queries regarding subscriptions, renewals, or gifts to: *Aperture* Subscription Service, 1-866-457-4603. For U.K. subscriptions, contact Falsten Partnership at subscriptions@falsten.com or call (020) 88062301.

Editorial contributions must be accompanied by return postage and will be handled with reasonable care; however, the publisher assumes no responsibility for return or safety of unsolicited artwork, photographs, book dummies, or manuscripts. When photographs or art submissions are requested by the publisher, any value for which *Aperture* could be liable must be agreed upon in writing in advance of delivery. If no agreement in writing is in effect, *Aperture* will not accept responsibility for the care or safety of material in its possession.

The Aperture Foundation's nonprofit status provides it with the independence and integrity fundamental to its efforts to publish, without compromise, the most significant work in photography. Individuals who wish to help maintain this vital force in photography may become Honorary Publishers ($10,000), Benefactors ($5,000), Patrons ($2,500), Donors ($1,000), Friends ($500), Sustaining Contributors ($250), Retaining Contributors ($150), or Contributors ($75). Names of contributors will appear in the May issue of *Aperture* magazine. Gifts are tax-deductible to the full extent of the law.

Copyright © 2003 Aperture Foundation, Inc. ISBN 1-931788-17-0

Library of Congress Catalog Card No.: 58-30845. Printed by Sing Cheong Co., Ltd., Hong Kong. Separations by Bright Arts (H.K.), Ltd., China.

TRANSFIGURATION
STEPHEN L. FELDMAN

MAY 2 - JUNE 13

FREDERICK BAKER INC.

1230 W. Jackson
Chicago, IL 60607
Ph (312) 243-2980
Fax (312) 243-4673
frederickbakerinc.com
MO-FR, 10 to 5 and by Appointment

PHOTO ECHO

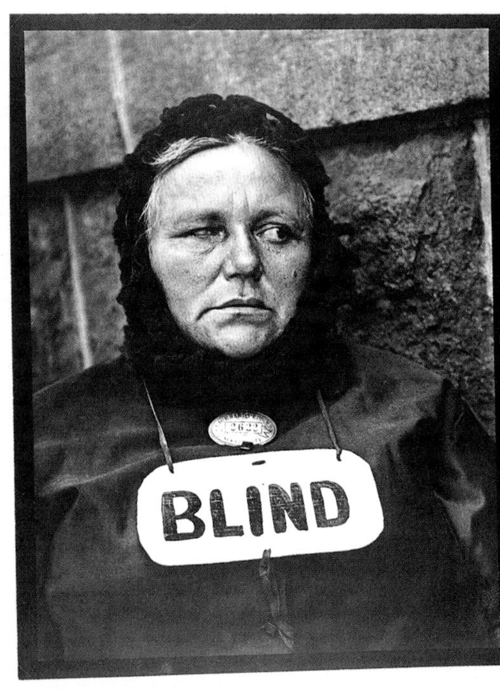

▲ Photograph by Marcos Vilariño.

◀Paul Strand, *Blind Woman*, 1917.

Do you have an idea for a Photo Echo? If so, we'd love to hear about it. If your submission is selected, you will receive a free one-year subscription to *Aperture*. Please send submissions to *Aperture* magazine, 20 E. 23rd St., New York, NY, 10010 Attn: Photo Echo.